52 easy-to-use
ASSEMBLIES
FOR MIDDLE & SECONDARY SCHOOLS

By the same author:

Teaching RE in Secondary Schools
52 Ideas for Secondary Classroom Assemblies
More Great Ideas for Secondary Classroom Assemblies

52 easy-to-use ASSEMBLIES
FOR MIDDLE & SECONDARY SCHOOLS

JANET KING

MONARCH
BOOKS

First published by Monarch Books 1999

ISBN 1 85424 432 9

Editorial office: Monarch Books,
Broadway House, The Broadway, Crowborough,
East Sussex TN6 1HQ

British Library Cataloguing Data
A catalogue record for this book is available
from the British Library.

Designed and produced for the publisher by
Gazelle Creative Productions,
Concorde House, Grenville Place, Mill Hill, London NW7 3SA.
Printed in Great Britain.

In memory of my Dad
who passed into the presence of the Lord
on 30 May 1997.

ACKNOWLEDGEMENTS

My special thanks to the following people for their invaluable contributions: Frank Acklin for his personal memories in 'Remembrance Day'; Matthew Britton for his original story 'Breakfast and The Blue Sky'; Olive Britton for researching some of the topics; David Hughes for ideas in 'Masks' and 'Welcome Friend', and Violet King for helping with the manuscript and providing inspiration on a number of themes. I would also like to thank Scarlett Kilden for the Easter prayer; Rose, Amy and Oliver Toye for their prayer on 'Journeys', and Will Toye for providing other material.

CONTENTS

* Denotes illustration

INTRODUCTION

The law concerning assemblies and acts of collective worship may change, but the onus is still on schools to provide pupils with opportunities for personal, moral and spiritual development through a variety of means. One of the main ways of meeting this need continues to be through a thoughtfully planned assembly programme, which takes into account the children's abilities and varied social and religious backgrounds as well as their personal needs.

Teachers and all those involved in managing and delivering an assembly programme constantly require stimulating, relevant and easy-to-use material which can be adapted to suit a variety of different situations. This book provides such material.

Each outline follows the same format:

- The focus, which provides a simple statement about the central theme of the assembly.
- A brief summary that explains the nature of the material.
- Information about any resources needed.
- A note about the amount of preparation required.
- The talk.
- Material for reflection or response.

- A 'thought' which may provoke further consideration or research.

All outlines are sensitive to the problems and difficulties schools experience in their quest to provide pupils with an appropriate assembly or act of worship in a school environment. At the same time, opportunities are given for pupils to question, reason and make up their own minds about the important issues raised through these assemblies.

A really great assembly does not usually just happen. Material like that provided in this book can be the starting point, but it cannot have life and real meaning unless the person using it brings to it their own ideas, unique style and sense of concern for every individual that will hear it.

I hope this book will provide busy teachers with plenty of good ideas as well as the stimulation needed to engage pupils in a meaningful dialogue with themselves, with others, and if they so choose, with God.

Janet King
Epping, June 1998

BIOGRAPHICAL NOTE
Janet has spent over twenty years in the classroom. She has been a head of department and a year tutor. She has experience of planning and leading assemblies and acts of worship in schools as well as writing materials for use in assemblies and RE. Janet now works full time as an independent consultant for RE and Assemblies.

1

<u>THEME</u>

Changes

FOCUS

Coping with change and changing for the better.

SUMMARY

This assembly could be used at the beginning of the school year when pupils may be changing classes or changing schools. It uses different people's experience of change to bring out the point that changes should be seen in a positive light and that it is up to us as individuals to make the most of it.

RESOURCES

Props for the mimes (ie umbrella, packet of crisps, apple, PE top and gym shoes, holiday clothes and suitcase, boxes, books, etc.).

PREPARATION REQUIRED

Run through with pupils doing mimes.

TALK

Most people don't like change. We like things to go on much as they always have, even though we know that most days bring changes of one sort or another. Here are some changes we all experience *(leader calls out each 'change' as different pupils come on to mime each change)*:

1. A change in the weather: Pupil mimes a sudden storm blowing up (shivers and puts up umbrella).
2. A change of clothes: Pupil mimes putting on PE top and gym shoes.
3. A change of diet: Pupil mimes eating a bag of crisps — another pupil comes along, takes away the crisps and hands over an apple.
4. A change of scene: Pupil walks on dressed for a holiday and carrying a suitcase.
5. A change of house: Pupil appears carrying a box, books, sports equipment, tapes, etc.

Some changes are more important and may cause us more concern than others. For example, changing house is more important than changing the family car or changing your hairstyle! Changing classes or changing schools is something we all face at different times. This can be quite scary, as well as exciting. Meeting new teachers or new pupils, changing classrooms or even changing schools can be a bit frightening or unsettling and it takes time to settle into new surroundings or a new routine, although most of us soon get used to it and settle down.

In 'First Day at Millington'[1] Jennifer Zabel describes Natasha and Simon Diddlewick-Clack's first day at their new school. Their father had just been appointed the headteacher and they would be moving from their present schools to join the pupils at Millington Comprehensive. They were on the threshold of a strange new world. Natasha was confident everything was going to be all right as soon as she got the school prospectus. It said that the uniform was cream and olive green and that it would go perfectly with her copper-coloured hair.

Simon wasn't so sure. He was more affected by newness and change. The first thing that caught Simon's eye as he made his way through the crowded corridors was the number of wooden wall lockers. Nine hundred and sixty two of them! His last school had been much smaller and his already shaky courage began to plummet. The second thing that struck him was the smell. It didn't smell a bit like his old school that had highly polished floors and creaking wooden staircases. Millington didn't smell of floor polish, in fact it didn't really smell of anything. He asked a group of boys that looked his own age where he might find his form room. He soon discovered they didn't have form rooms here. They were called tutor rooms. The boys watched as they sent Simon off up the stairs, and as he heard their laughter he realised that he had been 'had'.

Simon and Natasha had very different experiences and reacted in different ways to their first day at Millington. Simon couldn't wait for 3.30pm to come. 'What have you got to look so pleased about?' he asked Natasha grumpily as she came bouncing up to the car. 'Got yourself a new boyfriend, by any chance?' Natasha said she was happy because she had a fantastic English teacher and couldn't wait to get started on her project that had to be in by Friday. As for their father, his first day hadn't been too bad either. As their bottle green Rover made off down the road it was clear they were part of the Millington scene now, for someone had scrawled in the dust on the car boot, 'This car is dirty. Get it washed.'

REFLECTION/RESPONSE

Perhaps you are feeling a bit apprehensive this morning as you face some changes in your life or at school. If you are, try to see this as a new start and a fresh and exciting opportunity. Be determined that you will make the most of it and that this will be the start of something good.

TO THINK ABOUT

Life for most of us is a continuous process of getting used to things we haven't expected.

NOTES
1. Jennifer Zabel, 'First Day at Millington', *Memorable School Stories* (Octopus Books: London, 1980), p. 78.

2

THEME

Life as a Journey (1) Starting Out

FOCUS

Planning a special journey.

SUMMARY

This assembly is the first of four assemblies on journeys. It is about planning and preparing for a special journey and centres on the story of missionary Gladys Aylward and her plans for reaching China.

RESOURCES

A train timetable and selection of different maps including a map of the world. Optional — a sleeping bag, two hold-all bags, a passport, train ticket, Bible and two pretend £1 travellers' cheques.

PREPARATION REQUIRED

None.

TALK

Going on a journey can be very exciting. There are so many interesting places to visit and so many wonderful things to see, in this country and further afield. Many of you will have enjoyed a day in the country, a holiday at the seaside, a day trip to France perhaps or even a holiday abroad in another country. Part of the pleasure of going on a trip or a holiday is looking forward to it and getting everything ready. Plans have to be made, even if you are only going out for the day. There's food to think about — ('shall we take a packed lunch or get fish and chips?') and then you have to decide what to wear and what else you need to take for the journey.

You also have to think about how you are going to get there. For that, you may need a map or other sorts of information, depending on how and where you are going. If you are going by train (or tube) you may need one of these *(show train timetable or tube map and talk about how you would use it to plan the journey)*. If you are going by car, then a map would be useful *(show maps and how to plan a route)*. If you plan to go further afield — to France or another foreign country — then you would need to organise a plane ticket or channel crossing *(show ferry timetable or holiday brochure)*. Wherever you plan to go, preparations have to be made for the journey.

Imagine for a moment that you are going on a very special journey. You have wanted to go to this place for ages and you have been trying to persuade your parents that this is where they should take the whole family for your next holiday. Finally, they agree. It will mean saving hard, but if everyone helps then it should be possible. Imagine your excitement! Then it all goes wrong. Perhaps Dad loses his job or some unexpected expenses turn up. The trip is cancelled and there is nothing you can do about it — or is there?

Back in the 1930s a young lady called Gladys Aylward wanted to go to China. That is a long way as you can see from this map *(identify China on a world map)*. It would take quite a time to get to China even now, but when Gladys wanted to go, it was a very long and even dangerous journey. She believed that God was calling her to go and work in China as a missionary, but no missionary organisation was willing to send her and pay for her ticket to get there. Gladys had been a parlour maid and not had much by way of an education. She found studying difficult and had very little experience of Christian work. No one was interested in accepting Gladys as a missionary to China. Gladys was not going to be put off though. She was sure that God had chosen her to go to China and work for him there, so she prayed that God would help her find another way of raising the money to get there. She was very determined.

She took a job in London and decided to try to save up the money needed to get there by herself. She went to the nearest shipping office and asked how much it would cost for a single ticket to China. The booking clerk thought Gladys was joking, but she finally persuaded him that she was deadly serious. The clerk checked it out. The cheapest way to go would be by train and that would cost £47.10s. That was a lot of money then. The clerk advised her that it would be a dangerous trip because it would mean passing through Manchuria where there was a war going on. Gladys said that she would be the one taking the risk and asked if he would let her save up for the ticket. The clerk could see she was determined and finally he agreed.

Week by week, Gladys went to the shipping office with her shillings. She also wrote to a lady she knew in China, a Mrs Lawson, telling her of her plans. Mrs Lawson wrote back saying that if Gladys could make her way there, she would meet her in Tientsin.

The plan was now in place. Gladys continued to visit the shipping office until all the money was paid. She now had enough for the ticket *(optional — have a sleeping bag, train ticket, passport, two pretend £1 travellers' cheques and two hold-all bags to show while telling the last part of this story).*

There was a luggage limit on the train, so all Gladys could carry with her was a bedroll and two bags. Apart from this she had her ticket, her passport, a Bible and two travellers' cheques worth one pound each. With just this, she set off on her journey. She left Liverpool Street station at 9.30 am on Saturday 15 October 1932. Her journey to China had begun.

REFLECTION/RESPONSE

Perhaps you will never set out on a journey quite like the one Gladys set out on, but wherever and however you go, you will need to make the right kind of preparations for your journey. In the same way, we need to make preparations for our journey through life and we need to have the right things to take on our journey.

Let's think about the things that we will need as we prepare for our journey through life, as we reflect on the following prayer:

O Lord,
Guide us on our journey through this uncertain world. Give us consideration for others we meet and keep us from all evil and harm. Grant us your protection, that we may come safely to our journey's end. Through Jesus Christ our Lord. Amen.

TO THINK ABOUT

What special journey would you like to make and why?

NOTES

Charles Buckmaster, *Give us this day — Volume One* (University of London Press Ltd.: London, 1964), p. 45.

3
THEME

Life as a Journey (2) Help on the Road

FOCUS

God's help on our journey through life.

SUMMARY

This assembly is about recognising our need for help on our journey through life, especially when things get tough. Central to this assembly is the story of Wasyl Boltwin. Born in Siberia and brought up a communist, Wasyl faced many terrifying situations and more than once, he wanted to give up the struggle to survive. However, with God's help, he finally completes his journey and finds safety and peace of mind.

RESOURCES

None.

PREPARATION REQUIRED

None.

Wasyl never had life easy. He was one of fourteen children born to Ukrainian parents who lived in Siberia. There was never enough food for everyone and when Wasyl contracted typhoid at three years of age, his mother told his eldest brother to hide him away in a warm cupboard. Three days passed before anyone came to see if Wasyl was dead or alive. He survived this terrible ordeal and when he was old enough he was sent to the village communist school where he was taught that there was no God. The teachers told the children that if they saw or heard anyone praying they should come and tell them so that they could be taken away and re-educated. Some children did this and the people they reported were never seen again.

When he was sixteen, Wasyl was taken into the Red Army, although he was not given a uniform or any food. He was sent to the front line to fight against the Germans, but was soon taken prisoner. In such a cold climate, without proper clothing and food, many prisoners froze to death or died from illnesses related to these harsh conditions. Wasyl knew that unless he could escape, the same fate was waiting for him.

He managed to cut his way through the wire-netting surrounding the camp where the prisoners were being held, but he was soon caught and brought back. He was stood up against a wall and a soldier lifted his gun to carry out his execution, but another soldier intervened and stopped the shooting. Wasyl was disappointed not to die in some ways. He did not want to carry on living in these conditions.

The prisoners were moved on the next day and made to sleep in an open field. Wasyl and some of the other prisoners sought warmth and shelter in a hay rick, but the next morning at roll call some of the prisoners were missing. The order was given to set fire to the hay. Soldiers stood on top of the rick and shot at the men as they came running out of the hay. One soldier stood right on top of Wasyl, but again he escaped unharmed. As he lay there trembling, he wondered why his life had again been spared and if there really was a God who was protecting him. He thought that if this was true and he survived, he would spend the rest of his life serving him.

Eventually, Wasyl crawled out from his hiding place and walked away, but he had no idea which path to take or which direction to go. He saw a horse whip lying on the ground and he felt the urge to pick it up. As he did so, he heard the voice of a German soldier ordering him to stop right there. He had walked right into the German lines. The soldier saw the horse whip in Wasyl's hand and pointed beyond him to a horse and cart nearby. The soldier thought Wasyl was the driver of the cart that brought supplies to them, so he allowed Wasyl through. He walked as far as he could until his strength finally gave way. A lady saw him fall to the ground exhausted and ran from her cottage to help him. She had a boy of her own in the army and hoped that someone would also look out for him. Wasyl stayed at the woman's home until he got his strength back, then he went on his way knowing that the woman was in danger of being shot as a collaborator if he was found there.

Wasyl walked on until he came to a river. On the other side, Wasyl hoped to find some friendly soldiers, so he took off his clothes and plunged into the icy waters. He reached the other side, but his bundle of clothes had been washed away as he struggled to get across. Again he felt despair and wanted to die, but then to his surprise, he spotted his bundle of clothes caught up in reeds on the river-bank. He stayed in the forest for three days without proper food or shelter, then he saw a man cutting wood. The man was surprised to see Wasyl, but warned him that he was in danger there. The man took Wasyl home with him and he and his wife took him in and fed him, saving Wasyl's life. The family were Christians and shared their faith with Wasyl who by this time had become aware of the fact that there seemed to be a power greater than his own and that of the enemy, who was on his side and protecting him on his journey. He learnt that this power was God.

After the War, Wasyl kept the promise he had made when he was on the run. He determined to live the rest of his life and finish the journey he had started by serving the God who had guided, protected and brought him through so many dangerous situations.

REFLECTION/RESPONSE

Hopefully, none of us will have to make the kind of dangerous and difficult journey Wasyl did, but we all have different journeys as we go through life. Some are journeys we like making, others may be the kind of journey we would prefer not to make. The following prayer highlights some of the journeys we enjoy making and some that we don't like so much. Let's listen quietly as our readers pray for God's help and guidance on our journeys:

Reader 1: Lord God, we think about some of the journeys we make in our everyday lives. We think about some of the journeys that we enjoy making:
Reader 2: Going on holiday.
Reader 3: Visiting friends and families.
Reader 2: Going to church.
Reader 3: Going to the cinema.
Reader 2: Going out to dinner.
Reader 3: Going swimming.

All: Thank you, Lord, for these journeys.

Reader 1: These are journeys we don't enjoy making:

Reader 2: Going to the doctor.

Reader 3: Going to the dentist.

Reader 2: Going to hospital.

Reader 3: Going to school.

Reader 2: Going on a long journey.

Reader 1: Lord, help us on these journeys. We ask that whatever journeys we make, that you will be with us and guide us on our way.

Amen.

TO THINK ABOUT

You might like to think about and find out more about people like *Wasyl Boltwin* or *Gladys Aylward* who have made a long and difficult journey in order to help other people.

NOTES

My thanks to Rose, Oliver and Amy Toye for the prayer.

4

THEME

Life as a Journey (3) Helping Others Along the Way

FOCUS

Finding meaning in helping others.

SUMMARY

This is the third of four assemblies on the theme of Life as a Journey. This assembly centres on the idea of recognising that other people on the road can have needs greater than our own, and finding meaning, purpose and fulfilment in offering them a helping hand. It looks at Jaime Jaramillo's work among the street children of Bogota and encourages us to consider his example.

RESOURCES

Four students to read the story of Jaime Jaramillo. Optional — candle and matches.

PREPARATION REQUIRED

Practice readings with pupils.

TALK

Have you ever been on a plane journey? If you have, you probably found it an exciting experience, but people who are used to flying tend to get bored and on long flights passengers have to be distracted with frequent meals and in-flight entertainment. In a way, their lives are 'on hold' for the period of time that they are on the plane.

Some people spend much of their life in a similar sort of way — seeking to fill the time between birth and death with all kinds of pleasures and distractions like acquiring money, possessions and new friends. They put their lives 'on hold' in the sense that they fail to tackle or really get to grips with life's ultimate questions, choosing instead to live life without any real meaning or purpose.

Some people believe that life is a journey with purpose. Each person's journey is different because we all have different experiences that will affect us in different ways. How we treat others, how we choose to spend our time and money, how we react to other people along the way makes a difference to the kind of people we are and the sort of journey we will make.

Here is a story about one man who seemed to have everything one could wish for in life — a good job, plenty of money and a bright future. But one day he witnessed an incident that changed him and the direction he would take on his journey through life.

Reader 1: Jaime Jaramillo lives in the city of Bogota in Colombia. He is a prosperous oil exploration consultant whose company has contracts with the likes of Exxon and Chevron — a life of luxury is his for the taking. But walking home from work one night, just before Christmas 1973, he witnessed an incident which changed his life.

Reader 2: Bogota harbours a huge human tragedy — street children. Under the threat of death squads these children live in the only safe place available to them — the sewers. As Jaime walked home through the streets that night, he saw a small girl throw a toy box from a passing car. Two street kids dived for it. A little girl won the prize. She stood there smiling and Jaime smiled back. Neither of them had seen the truck. It hit her and she was thrown into the air. As the truck braked, it swung round and hit her again. The box she had raced to pick up was undamaged. It was also empty. She had died for nothing.

Reader 3: Jaime went home, disturbed and angry. He bought a Father Christmas suit and two hundred toys and went round handing the toys out. As he handed them out he felt a coldness in his heart, but he carried on. Each day he came across handicapped and sick children. Whenever necessary he would pay for hospital treatment. Before long he had three hundred children in five houses and he had found work for ninety-four former street kids. Encouraged by his success he established a foundation called 'Children of the Andes'.

Reader 4: His work in the sewers only began when a street kid pointed out to Jaime that many of his friends and contemporaries were now living there. Putting on breathing equipment he ventured below and began to find and rescue numerous children. Some of them were teenage mothers with newborn babies. Jaime describes the sewers with horrifying clarity:

Reader 1: 'You have to be very strong, physically and mentally. The smell is terrible, there are rats splashing all the time, mosquitoes and leeches and flying insects. You lose your strength because it's so slippery. You have to be careful not to fall, because you get that stuff in your mouth and you have diarrhoea for thirty days.'

Reader 2: Sadly some of the children are unaware of the many hazards that can afflict them: 'You see this froth. When it's flowing fast you get white froth and they think the water is clean. So they wash in it and then they get terrible infections, like gangrene.'

Reader 3: Tragically the children also face victimisation from vigilante gangs and death squads. Indeed, many Bogotans are offended by their existence and see them as vermin to be exterminated. Jaime, who is a committed Catholic, has fortunately been able to save three hundred and fifty children, although the work of the Andes foundation continues in its attempts to help the street kids who still seek safety and a home in the sewers of Bogota.

Reader 4: In spite of this heroic rescue of street children, it might surprise you to know that Jaime Jaramillo still appreciates the good life. He enjoys fine wine, eating out and dancing. He holidays in the Caribbean and Florida and when at home likes nothing better than sinking into his Jacuzzi with a glass of brandy!

Assembly Leader: When Jaime Jaramillo was confronted with the human tragedy of the Bogota street children, he did something constructive about it. He could have ignored the plight of these children, but he didn't. He realised that a good job, money and success was not enough. His work with the street children has helped him to find true meaning, fulfilment and a real purpose in life.

Perhaps there is a lesson here for all of us. There is no time for leaving our lives 'on hold'. It is time to take control.

REFLECTION/RESPONSE

As we light this candle *(light candle)* and remember the street children of Bogota and street children in other cities of the world too, you may like to reflect on the commitment of people like Jaime Jaramillo. You may wish to thank God for their work and pray that they will be an inspiration to you as you continue your own journey down the road of life.

TO THINK ABOUT

Perhaps this story has challenged you to find out more about projects like the Children of the Andes and put someone else's needs before your own. Perhaps you feel your life has been 'on hold' and now is the time to do something about it.

NOTES
Mark Roques, *The Good, The Bad and the Misled* (Monarch Publications: Crowborough, East Sussex, 1995).

5

Life as a Journey (4) Final Destination

FOCUS

Looking at life as a journey with a final destination.

SUMMARY

This is the last of four assemblies that look at the idea of life as a journey. It centres on the preparations and requirements for a journey to another country and then moves on to look at what Christians might call a travel guide for heaven.

RESOURCES

Two suitcases or rucksacks, travel brochure, passports, mock plane tickets, etc. An OHT of 'A Traveller's Guide to Heaven'.

PREPARATION REQUIRED

Two pupils could be asked to play the part of two friends going abroad. They will need the 'props' listed above and may like to dress appropriately with sunglasses, sun hats, etc. They will need to prepare a short sketch on the lines given below.

TALK

The assembly opens with the airport sketch. The two friends arrive at the airport carrying their luggage, tickets and passports. They engage in a conversation on the following lines:

Pupil 1: Have you got the tickets? I've got the passports here somewhere....

Pupil 2: 'Course I have. For goodness' sake stop panicking.

Pupil 1: All right. Keep your hair on. I was only asking. I don't know why I've brought so much stuff. This suitcase weighs a ton. Now where did I put my dollars?

(They sit down to sort themselves out.)

Pupil 2: (Pulling out travel brochure) I can't wait to get to Disneyland. The hotel looks great and the rides look brilliant. I can't believe we're finally on our way. Hey, look! Our flight number has just come up on the departure board. I think we should get to the check-in desk. I want to get a seat next to the window if I can.

Pupil 1: OK. Good idea. Once we've checked in we can get rid of our cases, go through customs and have plenty of time to look around the duty free. Come on — let's go.

(Thank the pupils for their performance.)
Planning for a holiday and going abroad is really

30

exciting — especially if you're going somewhere like Disneyland. But before we get to the stage of packing our bags and travelling to the airport, there is a lot of preparation to be done. First, you and your parents need to read up about the destination *(show travel brochures)* and find out all you can about the best place to stay, choosing the type of accommodation you want or can afford. Then you need to check if you need any inoculations or vaccinations. Some more exotic destinations require you to take malaria tablets, and this has to start well before you go. You will need some foreign currency if you are travelling abroad and you will probably need to take some travellers' cheques. As the day for departure gets close, you will have to sort out the clothes you need to take and think about what you are going to wear for the journey. You will then have to squeeze everything into your bag or suitcase and make sure you have the tickets and your passport. There is so much to think about, but if you don't get things organised properly, the whole thing could end in disaster.

Some people think of life rather like a journey. Like any journey, you need to know where you are going and have a good idea of how you are going to get there. Christians believe their ultimate destination is heaven and that the Bible is like a guidebook or travel brochure which sets out everything you need to know about how to prepare for and reach your final destination which they call heaven. This OHT highlights some of the main points from the Christian's travel guide — the Bible *(put up OHT)*:

A Traveller's Guide to Heaven

Accommodation: First class — 5 star, booked in advance.

'In my Father's house are many rooms...I am

going there to prepare a place for you' (Jesus' words in John 14:2).

Passports: Passports will be checked on entry and those not registered with the proper authority will not be allowed past the gates.

'Nothing impure will ever enter it, nor anyone who does what is shameful or deceitful, but only those whose names are written in the Lamb's [Jesus'] book of life' (Revelation 21:27).

Tickets: Your ticket is one way and a written pledge that guarantees your outward journey. It must be claimed and its terms and conditions met.

'Whoever hears my word and believes him who sent me has eternal life...and has crossed over from death to life' (John 5:24).

Departure times: The exact date of departure is unknown. Travellers should be ready to leave at short notice.

'It is not for you to know the times or dates the Father has set by his own authority' (Acts 1:7).

Customs: There is only one declaration required while going through customs:

'If you confess with your mouth, "Jesus is Lord", and believe in your heart that God raised him from the dead, you will be saved' (Romans 10:9).

Immigration: All passengers are classified as immigrants, since they are taking up permanent residence in a new country.

'They were longing for a better country — a heavenly one...for he has prepared a city for them' (Hebrews 11:16).

Luggage allowance: No luggage whatsoever can be taken.

'We brought nothing into the world, and we can take nothing out of it' (1 Timothy 6:7).

Vaccination: Injections are not needed as diseases are unknown at the destination.

'He [God] will wipe every tear from their eyes. There will be no more death or mourning or crying or pain' (Revelation 21:4).

Currency: Stocks of currency may be forwarded ahead to await the passengers arrival. No limit.

'Store up for yourselves treasures in heaven, where moth and rust do not destroy, and where thieves do not break in and steal' (Matthew 6:20).

Clothing: A complete and appropriate new wardrobe is provided for each traveller.

'He has clothed me with garments of salvation and arrayed me in a robe of righteousness' (Isaiah 61:10).

Reservations: Booking now open. Apply now.

'Now is the time of God's favour, now is the day of salvation' (2 Corinthians 6:2).

REFLECTION/RESPONSE

Pupils could be asked to think quietly about the journey they are making in life. Are they making the right preparations for it?

TO THINK ABOUT

Live today to the fullest! Remember, it's the first day of the rest of your life.

SONG IDEA

One more step along the road I go.

6
THEME

I've Started
So I'll Finish

FOCUS

Perseverance.

SUMMARY

This assembly compares some thoughts about the London Marathon and the aim to keep going and to finish the race with the need to persevere and keep going through the good and the bad times in life.

RESOURCES

Two pupils who are good runners and may have raced for the school or for charity to come to the front. They should be in their running gear or their games/PE kit with a number pinned on their vest — ready for a race. OHT of an athlete running a marathon.

PREPARATION REQUIRED

None, other than the above.

TALK

(Invite your two 'marathon runners' to come out. Explain that they are dressed like this because today's

*assembly is about running the race and the importance
of finishing it. You may be able to ask them about their
experience in running for the school or for their 'house'
as appropriate. Put up your OHT of a marathon runner.)*

Every year now, thousands of people apply to take
part in the London Marathon. In 1997, 100,000 people tried to get permission to run in the race. In the
event, about 41,000 were granted permission to take
part, so many thousands of people were disappointed.

The first London Marathon was staged in 1981
and it has now become an important event in the
British sporting calendar. The nice thing about this
race is that many people who are not professional
athletes can join with the 'serious' runners and experience the unique atmosphere of the race while raising money for a variety of charities and worthy
causes. Young and old, able-bodied and handicapped
people can compete side by side with Olympic and
world-famous athletes. All those who take part have
to be dedicated, training for months for the event in
the hope and expectation of completing the 26
mile, 385 yard course around the streets of London.

As well as the incentive of just finishing the race,
many people have the added incentive of raising
money for special causes. Since the race started in
1981, more than £55 million has been raised by
sponsored individual runners.

Millions of people watch the event on TV as well
as huge crowds that gather along the route to watch
the runners go by and cheer them on their way.
Some of the competitors wear fantastic costumes or
carry amazing 'props'. One pair of runners in the
1998 race were running inside a 'viking boat', some
were dressed as 'teletubbies' and there was the usual
array of 'chickens', 'animals' and cartoon characters.
Of course, none of these characters won the race,
but most of them crossed the finishing line and
raised a lot of money for their chosen charities at

the same time. Their main aim was simply to finish the race, complete the course and live to tell the tale!

Life itself is a bit like a race. We all start out at the same time (when we are born into this world) although we may finish at different times. Some people have long and eventful lives, others may find that their 'race' is a short one. The important thing is that we keep going and give of our best for however long the race lasts. All of us experience 'highs' and 'lows' along the way, but we should never give up the race itself. We should keep going to the finishing line and persevere, even when the going gets tough.

Magnus Magnusson presented the TV quiz programme *Mastermind* for many years. He was the one who put the questions to the contestants who had to take their turn in the famous black leather chair. If the time ran out in the middle of a question, Magnus would always say those famous words: 'I've started so I'll finish.' These words would be a good motto for any school pupil, student or anyone engaged in the journey of life. 'I've started so I'll finish.' Your homework may be taking you a long time to do, but don't give up! You may have set out on a task that seemed very thrilling when you started it, but now the novelty has worn off and you feel like giving up. Don't! Make sure that you finish what you started. Some people go through things in life which must make them feel like sitting down and giving up the race altogether, but they don't. Somehow they manage to keep going.

One person who never gave up was Squadron Leader Edward Howell. He was wounded in action and found himself confined to bed in a military hospital in Greece. He had been badly wounded in both his arms and they were now useless. There was no escape from the monotony of the long days and nights in the hospital surroundings and a feeling of desperation and hopelessness began to set in. The only way anyone in that prison hospital seemed to get any relief from their situation was to plan their escape, but with two useless arms, Edward knew that he could never join them.

Then one night, as he lay in bed watching the stars through the bars on his window, he felt that God was telling him that there was still hope. He must persevere and keep going. He felt as if someone had come into that room and switched on the light, and for the first time he was able to see things in a more positive way. He became more interested in what the other people in the hospital were doing and what they were going through and as he began to take his eyes off his own difficulties he became more content and more determined to carry on.

Then one day, he had an overwhelming feeling that he should make every attempt to get the rest of his body as fit as he could so that he too could make his escape from that hospital-prison. It seemed impossible. A high wall covered on top with broken glass surrounded the hospital building. How could he climb that with two useless arms? The idea would not go away, so Edward began to think about ways in which it might be possible. He was determined now not to give up. He began to investigate the wall and found that at one point a lower wall led up onto the higher wall. He worked out that if he could make his way up by this route without being seen or heard by the sentry, then he could put some padding over the broken glass on the top of the main wall and throw himself over.

He decided to have a go. There was no going back now. One morning, he stuffed his pockets full of clothing and woollen articles and made for the wall. When he reached the main wall he found it was too high to swing his leg over it. He couldn't think what to do now. His arms were still too weak and useless to be able to haul himself up that way. Then an idea came to him. He could put all the woollen things he had in his pockets on the glass on the wall then lie along it and roll over. That way, he wouldn't have to use his arms at all. He determined to have a try, but as he tried to manoeuvre himself onto the wall he lost his balance and rolled over it head first. To his amazement he found himself on the other side of the wall with his feet firmly on the ground. He hadn't even been injured by the fall. Edward felt that God had helped him make this amazing escape and that he was now free to live.

REFLECTION/RESPONSE

Many of the people who take part in the London Marathon do so despite terrible injuries and handicaps. They have to train very hard to be able to compete at all, but they also show the same kind of courage and perseverance in the face of difficulties that Squadron Leader Howell showed in making that daring escape. Squadron Leader Howell felt that God was helping him to make his escape and that he had given him the will to carry on even when things looked hopeless.

Let us determine to carry on even when things are difficult and we don't know how to face up to or cope with the future or the problems that come our way. Some of you may like to ask for God's help and guidance as you face the future and pray for special strength to help you finish what you've started and carry on until the task is complete.

TO THINK ABOUT

Can you find other stories about people who had the perseverance and courage to carry on even when things seemed to be against them?

NOTES

Adapted from Edward Howell, 'Over the Wall', in D.M. Prescott, *The Senior Teacher's Assembly Book* (The Blandford Press, London, 1955), pp. 128–130.

7

It's a Challenge!

FOCUS

Responding positively to life's challenges.

SUMMARY

This assembly looks at the subject of challenges, first in a light-hearted way but then more seriously. It asks pupils to accept the challenges life presents and respond to them in a positive way.

RESOURCES

Three sealed envelopes containing three different challenges that can be taken up in the assembly. Materials for the challenges. Three readers.

PREPARATION REQUIRED

Setting up the challenges. Hear the readers.

TALK

Have any of you seen the TV programme called *Don't Try This at Home*? Those who have will know that in this programme people are set a variety of challenges. They can choose to accept the challenge or they can walk away or leave it to an expert to carry it out. I have prepared some great challenges for some of you in this assembly. The question is, will you dare to carry them out? I have three sealed envelopes in my hand. Each envelope contains a different challenge. I need a volunteer to choose one of these challenges.

(If no one volunteers then you will have to select a suitable candidate. Invite them to choose one of your sealed envelopes. The challenges could be a mixture of more serious and fun challenges. Depending on time, you may be able to use more than one challenge. Here are some ideas for challenges):

1. *Complete 10 simple sums in 30 seconds. (These could be written up on a board or on an OHT. You will need a stop watch and a bell or a buzzer to signal 'time-up'.)*
2. *Sing a well-known nursery rhyme while gargling. (Jug of water, paper cups and things to mop up with will be needed for this challenge.)*
3. *Make an all-weather garment for a friend in 60 seconds using the materials provided. (For this you will need a second volunteer to act as the model, a stopwatch and a bag of suitable material for them to work with. This could include a dustbin liner, pair of scissors to cut holes in it for the head and arms, belt or strip of material to go around the waist, rubber gloves, plastic rain-hat, etc.) This could be more fun set as a competition with two pairs taking part and two bags of identical materials to work with.*

(Thank the pupils accepting the challenges and reward them with a chocolate bar.)

Leader: There have been several different challenge-type programmes on TV in recent years where celebrities or members of the public are set a challenge of some sort, but we don't have to take part in a TV programme to face a challenge. Most of us face challenges of one sort or another every day of our lives. We have to get up and get to school on time, complete a variety of tasks in the lessons, do the homework set for that day and carry out all the chores that are waiting for us when we get home!

Some people have faced some very difficult challenges that most of us will never have to confront in our lifetime. Here are some examples:

Reader 1: Clare Francis, 5 feet 2 inches tall and weighing just over seven stone, was the first British woman to take part in *The Observer* Single-handed Transatlantic Race in her boat 'The Golly'.

Reader 2: Dr Roger Bannister was the first man in the world to run a mile in four minutes. He said that the incentive to his running was to prove his ability to do something well, and to do it alone.

Reader 3: Anne Sullivan may not be so well known as the other two, but she was Helen Keller's nurse and tutor, teacher and constant companion. Helen Keller was both blind and deaf. After months of devoted work and despair, Anne made a wonderful breakthrough that resulted in Helen understanding the connection between objects, people and words. The word 'water' was the first word Helen understood and it was then that she realised that the things she could smell and feel had names. From there Helen went on to more difficult tasks, learning to speak, read and write, with Mrs Sullivan as her ears and eyes.

REFLECTION/RESPONSE
What a challenge and what an achievement! In all three of these cases, people set themselves a very difficult challenge and all of them achieved the things

they had set out to do. What challenges are you facing today? If you feel there are no great challenges in your life, perhaps now is the time to think about the kind of things you would really like to achieve. It doesn't have to be anything big to start with. Why not set yourself some realistic challenges — things that, with a little extra effort, you know you could achieve. Once you have got into the habit of setting yourself some goals, then you can increase the challenge by setting yourself some more difficult or long-term challenges. Dr Roger Bannister said: 'We all have ideals, and as we grow up we have the choice, whether to pursue them or to give them up.'

TO THINK ABOUT

What ideals or goals do you have? Are you prepared to pursue them?

NOTES
Roger Bannister in D.M. Prescott, *Readings for the Senior Assembly* (Blandford Press Ltd: London, 1965), pp. 167–169.

8

A Great Escape

FOCUS

Looking at how some people have escaped from life-threatening situations.

SUMMARY

The stories of the crash-landing of the plane carrying the Leeds United football team and the pilot rescued from his small plane which became caught in power lines form the basis of this assembly.

RESOURCES

None.

PREPARATION REQUIRED

None.

TALK

Within seconds of the BA 748 aeroplane taking off from Stansted Airport in Essex, the pilot, Captain John Hackett, noticed flames streaming from the right-hand engine. On board were forty-four passengers including the Leeds United football team who had chartered the plane to take them to and from their Premier League match with West Ham. With a fire in one engine, the pilot knew that regulations dictated that he should turn the plane around and attempt a proper landing. But Captain Hackett reasoned that within thirty seconds the engine would explode in mid-air and with about one and a half tonnes of fuel on board, a large explosion would have been disastrous. It would have turned the plane into a fire-ball. He decided that the only hope was to ditch the plane and crash-dive from about 150 feet in the hope that he could bring the plane down safely before the two-mile runway ran out. The plane hit the ground at high speed and slid off the end of the runway finishing up in grass with its tail in the air as its nose wheel buckled from the impact. The emergency services immediately sped into action and eight fire engines rushed to douse the flames. No one was seriously hurt.

The Leeds chairman Peter Risdale, who was on the flight, said afterwards that as the plane touched down the emergency exits were open next to him, but he turned round to go down the aisle in search of his thirteen-year-old son, Matthew. Battling against the flow of passengers going the other way towards the exit, he was persuaded to go back and was told that Matthew would be fine. As they made their way out over the wing of the stricken plane, Peter saw his son making his escape near the tail of the aircraft. Together they ran from the plane, knowing that there was every possibility that it would explode within seconds.

Afterwards, passengers recalled how they had seen the fire in the engine and could even feel the heat from the blaze as they were told to prepare for a crash landing. There was a smell of aircraft fuel and there were fears that the plane would explode. People prayed and braced themselves for the bumpy landing. It was dark and passengers were unsure of their surroundings. Were they going to hit houses as they attempted to land? They didn't know. After what some described as what seemed like an age bumping along the ground, the plane came to a stop. The explosion never came.

Captain Hackett was hailed as a hero. His quick thinking may well have saved the lives of his passengers and crew. Player David Weatherall said that he thought he would never see his family again. Leeds assistant boss David O'Leary, who was slightly injured in the crash, said later that it was a fantastic escape and a miracle that everyone got out alive. They may have lost the match against West Ham, but the team was in no doubt that they were the lucky ones that night.[1]

There are many stories about people who have had an amazing or even miraculous escape from a potential disaster. In another recent incident in the news, businessman Mike Warren was apparently commuting to his place of work in Seattle from his home in Silverdale the other side of Washington State's Puget Sound, when his Cessna 150L flew into power lines after an aborted landing at a Seattle airport. Warren had reportedly been coming in to land when he suddenly aborted his landing attempt and took a sharp left turn away from the runway, hitting the power line 200 yards from the control tower. His small plane was left dangling by one wheel sixty feet above the ground. The power was quickly cut off, but it was another four hours before rescue teams were able to rescue the pilot. As onlookers cheered and in front of live television, Mike was eventually plucked from his cockpit and lowered safely to earth. The pilot appeared unhurt, but was taken to hospital for a check-up. It was unclear whether the cause of the accident was pilot error or mechanical failure, but whatever the cause of the accident, Mike certainly had a very lucky escape.[2]

These two true stories illustrate how almost every day, people make the news headlines with their own personal escape stories. Most of us probably have our own escape stories of one sort or another, although they hopefully have not been quite so dramatic as these two incidents.

REFLECTION/RESPONSE

Christians believe that life itself is a bit like an escape story. The Apostle Paul, writing to Christians in Rome, warns them of the danger of passing judgement on others when they are guilty of the same kind of thing. He asks: 'Do you think you will escape God's judgement?' The book of Hebrews contains a similar warning: 'How shall we escape if we ignore such a great salvation?' The point is clear. There will be no escape from the consequences of our wrongdoing or our neglect of the gospel if we fail to take account of the way of escape offered to everyone through Jesus Christ.

TO THINK ABOUT

It would be stupid to ignore the help of the emergency services or those who were trying to help us escape from a potentially life-threatening situation. Christians believe that it is equally dangerous to ignore 'God's rescue plan' for the world, which is offered to everyone through Jesus Christ.

NOTES
1. Adapted from the article 'Our Hero', *The Daily Express* (Wednesday 1 April 1998), pp. 1–3.
2. See article 'High tension for pilot in power line tangle', *The Daily Telegraph* (Friday 10 April 1998), p. 16.

9

<u>THEME</u>

Danger!

FOCUS

Some dangerous situations.

SUMMARY

This assembly looks at two very different people's stories of how they coped with a dangerous situation and how, with God's help, they came through them.

RESOURCES

Two signs. One carrying the word 'DANGER' and the other saying: 'WARNING — KEEP OUT'.

PREPARATION REQUIRED

None.

TALK

(Have signs ready to show.)

Have you ever seen a sign like either of these? Where might you find a sign saying 'DANGER'? It could be on a cliff-top, by some road works, next to some high voltage cables or it could be warning you about a danger up ahead. What about this one?

'WARNING — KEEP OUT'? Where might you see a sign like this? Yes, in front of a derelict building, near a quarry or close to the railway track perhaps.

Some danger signs are more specific, like — 'Danger Mines' or 'Warning — Falling Rocks'. When there is a potential danger or hazard ahead, people sometimes put up a sign to warn people about it and to tell them to take extra care or keep well away. We can also get warnings about things that may be a danger to us like a gale warning or a health warning about contaminated food or drinking water.

Unfortunately, we do not always get a warning about dangers that may be coming up in our lives. We don't always know what dangerous situations may be ahead of us, so there may be no opportunity to do something about it or prepare ourselves for it.

It is in these kinds of situations that people sometimes experience a lucky escape or a sense that someone is looking after them. Some people learn something new about themselves or are made to face important questions when they find themselves in a dangerous situation. This is what happened to some people that we are going to hear about this morning.

The first story is about a woman who believes that her own life and the lives of her husband and family were saved because she reacted very quickly to what she believes was a warning from God.

The whole family of mum, dad and the four children had been out for the day in their minibus. Dad was at the wheel and the road was a little twisty and narrow in places. They were going at a reasonable speed, but they didn't know that up ahead the road narrowed rather dramatically as it went under a bridge. The bridge was also on a corner, so it was impossible to see anything coming the other way. Not knowing the road, they could not have known what lay ahead. Looking back on the event,

49

Margaret recalls that seconds before the bridge came into view, she sensed a voice saying to her, 'There is danger under the bridge.' This thought was so strong that she called out to her husband, who was driving, to slow down, repeating that 'there is danger under the bridge.'

Recognising the urgency in his wife's voice, David stepped on the brakes and came to a slow stop just as the bridge came into view. At that moment a lorry came hurtling under the bridge at quite a speed and in the centre of the road. It was too tall and wide to get through it any other way. If they had not slowed up when they did, they would have met the lorry head on under the bridge and they wouldn't have had a chance.

As it turned out, no one was hurt and the family went on to complete their journey without further incident. Margaret maintains to this day that the warning she received about the truck was a message from God and that if she had not taken it seriously and called out to her husband at that moment, they could all have been killed.

The second story is about a man who was working in a war-torn country in the East until quite recently. He was with an organisation that was trying to bring the message of Christianity to the people there and help them rebuild their lives which had been devastated by war. It was still a very dangerous place. Most days the sound of gunfire could be heard around the city and there were frequent mortar attacks and sniping. The hospitals were full of men, women and children who had been injured in the fighting and many continued to die on a daily basis.

One day, the aid worker was trying to get across the city when a burst of firing broke out. He jumped into a nearby ditch to try to get some shelter. In this kind of situation, anything could happen. It was then that he sensed that he was not alone in the ditch. Turning round he saw a man whom he did not recognise. He was not sure from the way he was dressed which side he was on either! The man spoke: 'Quickly, follow me. You can't stay here!' Although he was unsure who this person was, he sounded determined. Together they peered up over the ditch and made a run for a wall a short distance away. They fell over the other side of it just in time to look back and see a shell explode in the ditch — on the very spot they had been a few seconds ago. The aid worker turned to speak to the man who had insisted on his leaving the ditch, but he was nowhere to be seen. He had disappeared into thin air. The aid worker never found out who the man was, but, secretly, he believed it was an angel who had come to save him from what would have been instant death.

REFLECTION/RESPONSE

When we see signs saying 'DANGER' or 'KEEP OUT' it would be very stupid to ignore them, but some people do and they sometimes pay the consequence of their stupidity with their lives. The two people in our stories both found themselves in dangerous situations where they could easily have lost their lives, but they didn't. Some people would believe that God's hand of protection was on them or that there was a greater power looking out for them.

TO THINK ABOUT

Why do you think so many people say they have prayed for help when they have been in a dangerous situation?

10

<u>THEME</u>

Guidance

FOCUS

Ways of making decisions.

SUMMARY

This assembly looks at the ways some people make decisions or seek guidance. It encourages pupils to think about the way they make their choices and decisions in life.

RESOURCES

None.

PREPARATION REQUIRED

None.

TALK

People have different ways of making decisions. Some people consult their horoscope, some close their eyes and stick a pin in a list, some talk to friends and ask for their advice, some people are guided by their feelings while others weigh up the pros and cons and make a considered choice.

Some people seek guidance from God or a spiritual leader. There are many examples of people who felt God showed them very clearly what he wanted them to do in a particular situation.

One such man was an Israelite called Gideon. We read about him in the book of Judges in the Old Testament. The story tells us that they were difficult times for Gideon and his people. The armies of the Midianites and the Amalekites, along with other tribes from east of the River Jordan had crossed over the river and were camped out in the Valley of Jezreel. It was clear that they were planning a major attack against the Israelite people. Gideon felt that the Lord was calling him to get his people together ready to resist such an attack. So he sounded a trumpet blast to call together the men of Abiezer who were willing to follow him. He then sent words to the tribe of Manasseh, requesting that they should come and join them along with the fighting men of the tribes of Asher, Zebulun and Naphtali. They all came together to prepare for battle under Gideon's leadership.

Gideon knew that God had promised to use him to save the Israelites, but as he faced the fight of his life, he asked God to give him a sign that he really would be with him and help him to meet the challenge that lay ahead. 'You promised me you would use me to save Israel,' Gideon said 'Now please do something for me. I will put out a piece of wool on the threshing floor. Tomorrow morning let the dew only be on the wool and not on the floor around it. Then I will know for sure that your promise to use me to save Israel is true.' And that was exactly what happened. The next morning, when Gideon got up, he found the wool was wet with the dew. He squeezed a whole bowlfull of water out of the wool, but all around it the floor was completely dry.

Gideon asked God for one more sign. This time he prayed that when he put the wool out that night, he would find it dry the next morning, but the floor around would be wet. This was what happened. Now Gideon was sure that God wanted to use him to save Israel.[1]

Still today, Christians believe that God can guide them and help them to make the right choice or important decision. One couple who believe they have experienced such guidance is Graham and Judy Nichols. They felt that God was calling them to take over the leadership of a small chapel in Wiltshire. It would be a big step for them, as it would mean Graham giving up his teaching job and the whole family moving. They decided the best thing to do would be to take up an invitation from one of the chapel members to go and stay in the village for a few days. Perhaps the way ahead would become clearer then. Graham spent some time up in their room praying about what he should do. As he was praying, he felt that God was speaking to him and showing him the way ahead. He read the verse from the Old Testament in the book of Ezekiel where it says: 'Get up and go out to the plain, and there I will speak to you' (Ezekiel 3:22). This verse seemed to leap off the page as Graham read it. He rushed downstairs to find his host, John. 'Where can we go and stand on the plain, a place that's near a river and overlooking Potterne?' he asked. John got out his map. 'Here,' he said, 'it's about ten minutes away.' They got in the car. It was very foggy out and it was dark. They drove onto part of Salisbury plain and to the place John had indicated on the map. They stopped the car and got out. The sky was clear now and they could see across the valley. As they looked, they could see a tall column of fire reaching about 100 feet into the air. The fog seemed to be wrapped around it and a bright light came and shone on it for about a minute.

It was a strange sight, but what did it mean? The

fire was real enough and the army training ground was close by, so that could explain the light. For Graham, it was a clear sign of God's guidance. He believes that God was showing him that he was meant to live and work in the valley below, but that there would be times when things would be hard and it would be difficult to see the way ahead through the fog. Graham became the pastor of the Potterne chapel on Valentine's Day 1998.[2]

REFLECTION/RESPONSE

Do you believe God can guide people to take a certain job or direction in their life? Those of you who do might like to take the opportunity to think about and/or pray for God's help and guidance through life in a few moments of quiet reflection.

TO THINK ABOUT

What advice would you give someone thinking about a change of direction in life?

NOTES
1. Adapted from Judges 6:33–40.
2. Adapted from 'Guided by Fire' in *New Christian Herald* (30 May 1998), p. 9.

11
THEME
Faith and Belief

FOCUS

Understanding the meaning of faith and belief.

SUMMARY

This assembly uses the story of Blondin the tight-rope walker to illustrate the real meaning of what it is to have faith or trust in a person and in God.

RESOURCES

OHT of the Blondin sculpture.

PREPARATION REQUIRED

None.

TALK

If you are familiar with the city of Birmingham, then you may have seen this metal sculpture which stands near one of the busiest roads leading out of the city *(display OHT)*. This sculpture, by artist Paul Richardson, shows a man in a very distinctive pose and holding a long pole. That is because he is a funambulist (tightrope walker to you and me) and a very famous one. He is a Frenchman called Charles

Blondin who is probably most famous for walking across the Niagara Falls on a tightrope — pushing a wheelbarrow. What a lot of people don't know is that he has a Birmingham connection, for not only did he walk across the Niagara Falls on a tightrope, but he also walked across the Edgbaston reservoir!

The story goes that Blondin set up his tightrope across the reservoir, but the rope was very slack and almost touching the water in the centre of the reservoir. Blondin set off on his walk across the reservoir and all went well until he neared the middle. Here, the rope was so close to the water that, with Blondin's weight on it, it actually began to dip below the surface of the water. The nearer Blondin got to the middle of the reservoir, the lower he sank into the water, until all that could be seen of him was the plume on his hat! But he kept on walking and eventually surfaced again and safely completed his walk to the other side.

The story that really made Blondin famous though, is the story of how he crossed the Niagara Falls on 15 September 1860. Blondin set his tightrope up 160 feet above the Falls. It was 1,100 feet long and spanned the entire width of the Falls. Huge crowds gathered to watch Blondin attempt one of the most amazing stunts the world has ever seen. Taking his pole in his hand to help him maintain his balance, Blondin mounted the rope as the people below and on the other side of the Falls waited with baited breath. Once he had settled himself, he set off on his amazing walk and crossed safely to the other side.

As the cheers died down, Blondin prepared himself for the return walk. This time, he decided it would be different and even more fantastic. He produced a wheelbarrow which he intended to push across the Falls, and asked for a volunteer to ride in it! The crowd fell silent. They had seen Blondin make that first crossing and they were sure he could do it, but no one was prepared to risk it! Then, one man stepped forward and offered to go. It was Henry Colcord, Blondin's assistant and manager. He, more than anyone, knew what Blondin was capable of and he was willing to put his life in his hands. Back they went across the Falls. They reached the other side safely once more. The crowds went wild. They knew that they had witnessed one of the really great stunts of modern times.

REFLECTION/RESPONSE

Imagine for a moment that you had been in the crowd that day watching Blondin cross the Niagara Falls. How do you think you would have reacted to his invitation to be pushed back across the Falls in a wheelbarrow? Would you have volunteered? You had seen him go across safely the first time and if you agreed to go with him back across the Falls, no doubt your name would go in the history books too!

Why was it that no one wanted to go? They all believed that Blondin could do it, but no one (except his assistant) was willing to put their beliefs into action and trust Blondin to carry them safely across.

Some people are like this about other beliefs. They believe in God, they may believe that Jesus is the Son of God, but they are not prepared to put their beliefs into action and do anything about it. Consequently, their faith never really 'gets off the ground' and they stay on the edge of the Falls without ever knowing the excitement of placing themselves in the hands of the 'master' and going across to the other side.

There are many modern examples of people who did take the risk and put their lives in God's hands and struck out across the river. Terry Waite is someone you may have heard of whose personal journey of faith led him to work as a special envoy for the Archbishop of Canterbury. He successfully negotiated the release of several people who had been taken hostage in different parts of the world, but ended up being captured himself while trying to secure the release of hostages in the Middle East. He spent much of his time as a hostage in solitary confinement and was subjected to torture and years of suffering, but through it all, Terry never lost his faith or doubted his Christian beliefs. He claims that it was his faith that helped him through that terrible experience and that those whose faith has been applied and tested are 'fortunate, if not always comfortable'. They are fortunate, he says, 'because they will look forward to resurrection, but more — they will *know something of it in their own experience.*'

TO THINK ABOUT

What things are very important to you and what or who do you put your trust in?

NOTES
1. Terry Waite, *Footfalls in Memory* (Coronet Books, Hodder and Stoughton, London, 1995).

ACKNOWLEDGEMENT
My thanks to Paul Richardson for permission to use the line drawing of his sculpture of Blondin.

12

THEME

Bread, Cheese and a Bag of Corn

FOCUS

Small start — big finish! Accepting a challenge.

SUMMARY

This assembly takes as its basis the well-known Bible story of David's visit to his brothers that ends with David fighting Goliath. It encourages pupils to see how a humble start can turn into an exciting challenge.

RESOURCES

A bag in which you have hidden a piece of cheese, a small loaf of bread or a roll and a bag of popcorn.

PREPARATION REQUIRED

Some pupils for the dramatic reading.

TALK

Today's assembly is about big things coming from small beginnings. It takes as its basis a story that many of you may have heard before. It starts with a young boy being sent off to take supplies to his Israelite brothers who are engaged in a local war with the Philistines, their old enemy. In this bag *(show bag)* I have some clues to the supplies he was instructed to take with him. According to the Bible story, David was given 125 pounds of corn *(show popcorn)*, 10 loaves of bread *(show bread or roll)* and 10 cheeses *(show cheese)*. He had the task of transporting all this to his brothers who were holed up with the fighting men of Israel and King Saul, their leader, in the valley of Elah. They weren't going anywhere. They were terrified out of their wits by the power of the enemy and their champion fighter, a giant of a man named Goliath. Here's what happened next.

Narrator: Imagine the scene at the army camp as David marches in, dragging a load of corn (it was getting heavier by the minute), 10 loaves of bread (not quite so fresh now) and his ten (slightly sweaty) cheeses.

David: Hi guys! Got some grub for you. What's going down?

Eliab: Not a lot. Come on. Hand over the nosh.

David: OK. Take it easy. What's that giant of a bloke shouting about?

Eliab: Oh, take no notice, he does that every day.

David: Why doesn't someone pick up his challenge and take him on?

Eliab: Are you serious? Have you seen the size of him? Anyone would be mad to go out there. If you've just come to stir things up, you might as well get back to your sheep right now. Who's looking after them anyway?

David: Now what have I done? Can't I even speak?

Narrator: As you can see, it didn't take long for the boys to be at one another's throats.

Eliab: You always were a big head. Perhaps you fancy a one-to-one with him.

David: Why not? I've killed a lion and a bear with my sling-shot. If God is on my side, what's there to be frightened of?

Narrator: Pretty soon, word got around the camp that a boy was offering to take Goliath the Philistine giant on. The king heard it on the grapevine. He asked to see young Dave.

King Saul: What's all this then? I hear you're willing to go out and face the giant. Where's your CV? Have you done this sort of thing before?

David: Not exactly, but with the God of Israel on my side and the target practice I've had while looking after the sheep, I'm prepared to give it a go.

King Saul: If you're sure... better wear my suit of armour and take my sword.

Narrator: King-size armour — won't fit. Sword's too heavy. Not a good idea.

David: If you don't mind sire, I think I'll keep the jeans and the sling. I'm used to that you see. Killed a lion and a bear....

Eliab: All right. We've heard it all before.

Narrator: So David went just as he was. The only weapon he had was his sling. So he went down to the stream in the bottom of the valley between the enemy camps and picked up five smooth, round stones. Now he was ready to face Goliath.

David: Say your prayers, Goliath. Your number's up! I've got the God of Israel fighting with me.

Goliath: What's this? Am I a dog that you come out to fight me with sticks? What a joke! Come on then. What's keeping you?

Narrator: The Israelites and Dave's brothers held their breath. Shouldn't be long now. Look out! There's the first of David's stones on its way. Hope it's on target.

David: Rock on Goliath. I've got a message for you from the God of Israel.

Goliath: Ahhh! What the…? *(Falls to the ground.)*

Narrator: Looks like Dave's on target. Got him right between the eyes. Time to finish the job.

So there you are. And it all started with a sack of corn *(hold up popcorn)*, some bread *(hold up loaf)* and some cheese *(hold up cheese)*, but it led to the Israelites winning a great victory over their enemies.[1]

REFLECTION/RESPONSE

It's true that big things can come from small beginnings. Let us be silent for a few moments and think about the story we have heard. Perhaps you have what looks like a mountain facing you and you don't know how you are going to climb it. Let this story inspire and encourage you. David was too young to be in the regular army, but he wasn't afraid to tackle the giant, secure in the knowledge that God had helped him in the past and was with him now. He faced the giant with confidence and 'took him out' with one shot.

TO THINK ABOUT

Have you got some giants in your life that need 'taking out'?

NOTES
1. Based on the story of David and Goliath in 1 Samuel 17:17–37.

Luck or Design?

FOCUS

Do things happen by chance or is there a 'master plan'?

SUMMARY

This assembly raises the issue of whether things happen to us by chance or whether there may be more to it than just luck.

RESOURCES

Home-made bran tub.

PREPARATION REQUIRED

A bran tub can be prepared using a suitable container and polystyrene chips like those used for packing purposes. An assortment of good and not so good prizes should be wrapped up and placed in the tub.

TALK

Some of you will probably have been to a school fête or summer fair and seen a bran tub or lucky dip rather like the one I have here *(show tub)*. The idea is that you pay your money (probably something like 50p) and then you take your choice by selecting a surprise package from the tub. You might win something good, or you might not! Would anyone like to come out and have a free go at my bran tub? *(Select two or three people to have a go.)* Of course, a lot of the fun is in just having a go in the hope that you might win something worth while. There are plenty of other exciting games that require a certain amount of luck if you are to win anything worth having. At some fairs there is a game where you fish plastic ducks out of the water and the number painted underneath the duck determines your prize, or you may have to guess the weight of a cake or decide how many beans there are in a jar, etc. Most of these types of games are games of chance where no real skill is involved.

One highly popular game of chance, that a lot of people play every week now or even twice a week, is the National Lottery. People buy their tickets and pick their winning numbers. The chance of winning a big prize is very small, but a lot of people find it exciting to check their numbers against the winning numbers every week. Some people claim they have a special system for picking their numbers, others choose family birthdays or anniversary dates. For most people, it is just a bit of fun and they like the excitement of checking out their numbers every week. Of course, somebody has to win, but the chances that 'it could be you' are very slim.

Every now and again, one hears stories about someone who claims that winning the lottery was no accident. It was all part of a plan. One man was facing bankruptcy because his haulage firm was thousands of pounds in debt and on the verge of collapse. When Harry went out to buy his lottery ticket that week, he decided to stop off at the local church to pray that this time he would be lucky. He was desperate. When he got to the church, he found the doors were locked, so he just stood in front of them and prayed for a lottery win. 'Please God, let me win.' It was a last desperate cry for help. Harry then went straight to the shop to buy his ticket. His wife picked the winning numbers using mostly their children's ages. As the numbers were given out that night, they realised that some of them seemed familiar. It was only later, when they got home, that they discovered they had all the winning numbers. They shared the jackpot winning £2.6 million.

A few days later, Harry returned to the church to give thanks for his win. He spoke to the vicar there, who was not impressed by Harry's story. He was not convinced that Harry's win had anything to do with God or Harry's prayers. The vicar said later that he did not approve of the National Lottery and that he did not support gambling. Many Christians would agree with this view, but that didn't stop Harry and his wife celebrating their good fortune.[1]

REFLECTION/RESPONSE

Do you think God heard Harry's prayers and stepped in to help Harry win the Lottery? Not all churches are opposed to the Lottery or other forms of gambling, although most Christians believe that the things that happen to us in life do not all happen just by chance. There are several references in the Bible to the idea that God has a plan for our lives and that he takes a special interest in everything we do. Paul, writing to the church in Ephesus, reminds the Christians there that they have been chosen by God according to the plan of him who works out everything in line with the purpose of his will.[2] If this is true, then some things that happen to us can't just happen by luck, can they?

TO THINK ABOUT

Do you know of other stories about people who have prayed and had their prayers answered?

NOTES
1. Adapted from the story 'Wad from God', *The Sun Newspaper* (2 October 1996).
2. See Ephesians 1:11.

14

<u>THEME</u>

Take-away

FOCUS

Thinking about the things pupils might take away with them from school into life.

SUMMARY

This assembly invites pupils to think about some of the important things they learn in school and through their contact and interaction with others. It also looks at some Christian principles they may take with them into life.

RESOURCES

The remains of a 'Happy Meal' or similar.

PREPARATION REQUIRED

None.

TALK

I expect most of you have had one of these at some time *(show 'take-away' meal box, and examine the contents)*. When you buy one of these you get more than a drink, hamburger and chips. You get a toy as well *(show toy)*. There are lots of other types of take-away meals you can get, like fish and chips, a Chinese or Indian meal or pizza. Perhaps you sometimes have a take-away meal at home as a special treat. Some people like to relax at the weekend by watching a video and sending out for a 'take-away'. It's easy and most of us enjoy a 'take-away' meal.

As well as 'take-away' meals there are lots of things that we can 'take away' in life. In school, for example, we learn many things that we can take with us through life. We learn to read, to add up and take away, we learn facts about things that happened in the past and we learn many skills that will help us cope with all sorts of tasks and situations as we go through life. The teachers we remember most after we have left school are the ones who have helped us to make the most of the skills and talents that we have and put everything we can into what we do.

This is something a young boy who had a very special gift for music learnt from his teacher. He had taken lessons from various piano teachers, but they did not have the skills or ability to take the boy further. Then, the boy's parents heard about a famous piano teacher who was retired and was no longer taking pupils. In desperation they went to see this wise old man and pleaded with him to take their son on as his pupil. The teacher didn't want to take any more students now, but when he heard the boy play, he realised that he had a very special talent and finally he agreed to take the boy.

The years passed quickly, but the old music teacher taught the boy more than the rudiments of music. He poured his spirit and his passion for music into the boy and taught him that music is like the readable script of life and that it was life itself expressed through different tones on a musical instrument. Gradually the boy began to understand that there was more to being a great pianist than

71

making sounds with his fingers. He realised that he needed to pour his whole being into his music and let it flow out through his fingers as he played.

Finally, the day came for the boy to give his first real public performance. The teacher felt that he was now ready to show his talent to the world. Word spread that the boy had great promise and on the night of the performance the hall was full. As the boy sat down at the piano to play, a hush fell over the audience. He leaned over the keyboard and started to play. He poured his very soul into the music. As he played, people were visibly moved by his music. It was so beautiful that some people even wept as they listened to it. As he finished, people threw flowers and money onto the stage, but the boy did not look at the audience, his eyes were firmly fixed on the balcony where his old teacher sat. To his delight, the old man was nodding in approval and whispering, 'Well done, lad. You're on the right track. Keep it up!'

We can all learn a lesson from this which we can take away with us into our own lives. We need to listen and learn from people who know what we are capable of and have the ability to draw out the best from us. We need to learn how to put our 'heart and soul' into things that are worth doing. If we learn to do this, we will know true success.

REFLECTION/RESPONSE

Here are some thoughts from an unknown writer on things we need to think about taking time for as we go through life:

Time is for work, it is the price of success.
Take time to think, it is the source of power.
Take time to play, it is the secret of youth.
Take time to read, it is the fountain of wisdom.
Take time to be friendly, it is the road to happiness.

Take time to dream, it's hitching your wagon to a star.
Take time to love, it is the highest joy in life.
Take time to laugh, it is the music of the soul.

Which three qualities would you choose to take away with you if you were asked to choose from this list?

TO THINK ABOUT

What qualities would you advise a friend to take with them through life?

15

Neighbours

FOCUS

What it means to be a good neighbour.

SUMMARY

This assembly begins with two 'neighbours from hell' stories and moves on to look at the 'good neighbour' story from the Bible — the good Samaritan.

RESOURCES

Copies of the stories and the sketch for readers. OHT of the Bible references for reflection.

PREPARATION REQUIRED

Practice for the readers.

TALK

There have been a number of programmes on TV recently about people who have fallen out with their neighbours or had a bad experience with builders. The 'Neighbours from Hell' programmes were followed up with a 'Builders from Hell' series. It is amazing what some people have to go through because of nuisance neighbours or 'cowboy' builders. The following stories show what can happen when things get out of hand.

Reader 1: There is a particular family, all living quite close to one another in the Nottingham area. Two of the brothers, now grown up and married with families of their own, had never got on well even when they were young, but sibling rivalry has now grown into all-out war. Apart from verbal abuse, there have been stone throwing incidents and paint daubed over one of the brother's car. As if this wasn't enough, one of the brothers attacked the other one with a plank of wood, beating him about the head and chest. There seems to be no hope of reconciliation even though their elderly parents and their own families are at the point of despair.

Reader 2: Most disputes with neighbours are to do with noise — blaring music, doors slamming and endless rows. Another case, reported in *The Daily Mail*, went even further. According to this report, a father of five's actions drove a neighbour to suicide. This is not just a story of a man who played his music too loudly, had fights with his girlfriend in the street and hurled abuse at people after bouts of drinking. He has driven neighbours mad with fear and sleeplessness. A confessed thief who has served a prison sentence, he became a living nightmare to his neighbours. One neighbour reported that he had broken down his own front door on two occasions and eventually drove the other neighbour to commit suicide because he couldn't cope with all this.

(Thank the readers.)
There are many other stories about people who were good neighbours. Jesus told one in response to a young lawyer who asked him the question: 'Who is my neighbour?' The story goes something like this:

Reader 1: A certain young Jew with a liking for the law,

Reader 2: Asked Jesus a simple question:

Reader 1: What must I do to get eternal life?

Reader 2: Jesus answered his question with another question:

Reader 1: What is written in the law?

Reader 2: Love God and love your neighbour as yourself

Reader 1: The man answered.

Reader 2: Quite right — do this and you will live for ever

Reader 1: Jesus replied.

Reader 2: Not wanting to look silly

Reader 1: The lawyer pretended he didn't know who his neighbour was

Reader 2: So he said: who is my neighbour?

Reader 1: How long have you got? Said Jesus

Reader 2: Knowing how much an hour a lawyer charges.

Reader 1: I'll answer your question with a story.

Reader 2: Jesus said:

Reader 1: A Jew who got beaten up and robbed

Reader 2: Was left by the road to die.

Reader 1: A priest happened to go that way, but he didn't stop.

Reader 2: Another religious man also went by,

Reader 1: But he didn't stop either.

Reader 2: At last a Samaritan

Reader 1: A foreigner, whose people didn't get on with the Jews,

Reader 2: Went that way. He stopped,

Reader 1: Looked at the man and decided to help him.

Reader 2: He bound up his wounds the best he could

Reader 1: Put the man on his own donkey

Reader 2: And took him to a local inn.

Reader 1: He even left money with the innkeeper

Reader 2: To pay him for looking after the man.

Reader 1: Now, said Jesus to the lawyer,

Reader 2: Which of these men acted like a good neighbour?

Reader 1: It didn't take a brilliant lawyer to work that one out.

Reader 2: The one who helped him, the lawyer replied.

Reader 1: Exactly, said Jesus.

Both Readers: Go and do the same yourself.

REFLECTION/RESPONSE

Our neighbours are the people we meet and work with in school (pupils and teachers), our friends and anyone who needs a helping hand.

The idea that everyone we meet should be treated in a 'neighbourly way' is not limited to Christian tradition, but the Bible is full of instructions on how to behave toward our neighbours and everyone we meet. Here are some of them. *(OHT)*

EVERYBODY NEEDS GOOD NEIGHBOURS

Some Bible passages for reflection:

'Do not defraud your neighbour or rob him' (Leviticus 19:30).

'Love your neighbour as yourself' (Leviticus 19:18).

'Do not plot harm against your neighbour, who lives trustfully near you' (Proverbs 3:29).

'Love does no harm to its neighbour' (Romans 13:10).

'Speak truthfully to [your] neighbour' (Ephesians 4:25).

'Love your neighbour as yourself' (James 2:8).

TO THINK ABOUT

What kind of neighbour are you?

SONG IDEA

When I needed a neighbour, were you there?

16

A Bit of a Balancing Act

FOCUS

Getting our priorities right.

SUMMARY

This assembly focuses on the need to think about the various things that fill our lives and take up our time in different ways. It suggests that we need to think about getting things in proportion and sorting out our priorities. A practical activity demonstrates the problem and offers a way into the main talk.

RESOURCES

1. A number of boxes clearly labelled with the following words:
   SCHOOL, HOME, FAMILY, HOMEWORK, RECREATION, RELATIONSHIPS, SPIRITUAL LIFE, MONEY.
2. Suitable objects for pupils to try their hand at balancing (eg broom, plastic plates, etc).

PREPARATION REQUIRED

Labelling of boxes — practice at balancing objects! Find out if there are any pupils who have learnt balancing skills. They might be willing and able to show off their skills in the assembly.

TALK

Have you ever been to a real circus and seen some of the great balancing acts there? If not, you will have seen plenty of balancing acts on TV. Some people can balance all kinds of things on their head, on their feet or both — and juggle at the same time! Others perform amazing balancing tricks on the high wire or tightrope or troops of acrobats do all sorts of acrobatic stunts and balancing acts.

How good are you at balancing things? Invite some pupils out to try their hand at balancing the various objects you have brought for that purpose. If you have found some pupils who have real balancing skills call them out to demonstrate these briefly to the rest of the group. Suggest that life itself is a bit of a balancing act. Hold up the first of your labelled boxes (eg SCHOOL) and talk about the amount of time we spend in school during term time. Invite a volunteer to come down and hold the box with the label towards the pupils so it can be seen. Go through each of the ways we might spend our time and invite another pupil to come out to help pass on the boxes to the pupil who has to try to balance all of them — on their head, under their arms, etc. Don't worry if they drop them — that will only reinforce your point that it is very difficult to balance all these things and get our priorities right. Give an example of how we might get it wrong sometimes — like spending too long watching TV when we should be doing homework or spending too long out with our friends when our family might need us or there are important jobs to be done around the house.

Suggest that we need to get our priorities right. It is hard to do everything we want to in the way we would like. There are simply not enough hours in the day. Sometimes we let our own plans get in the way of our family, or friends get in the way of our school work and everything gets in the way of our spiritual life! We simply have no time to sit down and reflect for a moment on things that may have eternal or lasting consequences. There is no time for God in our lives. Life can be a bit of a balancing act.

Occasionally something momentous happens, such as a loved one or someone close to us getting sick or even dying. It can take a long time to recover from this and it seriously knocks us off balance. Other things like a bad test result or the cancellation of our plans can affect us more than it should, clouding our judgement and causing us to lose our sense of perspective. Occasionally, it is good to take time out to reflect on the way our lives are going.

This is probably what the writer of the book of Ecclesiastes had in mind when he said, 'There is a time for everything and a season for every activity under heaven' (Ecclesiastes 3:1). Jesus also knew that there were times when his disciples needed to stop working, take some time out and keep a sense of balance in life.

REFLECTION/RESPONSE

You may like to spend a few moments thinking quietly about the way you divide your time at the moment between different activities. Is your life balanced? Do you leave enough time for the things that really matter? You may like to focus on one of the things that takes up a lot of your time and attention and ask yourself if you should be spending so much time on this aspect of your life. You may like to pray that God will help you to get a proper balance between the important areas in your life.

TO THINK ABOUT

Mastering any skill, like balancing things, requires time and concentration. Which area of your life might be improved by spending more time on it this week?

17

<u>THEME</u>

Bully!

FOCUS

The harm that bullying can do.

SUMMARY

This would make a good assembly for a class to do as it involves a number of people. It focuses on the dangers and distresses caused to people who are bullied. It includes a true story about Kelly who was driven to suicide because of bullying and a sketch showing what happened to one bully who didn't get away with it in the end.

RESOURCES

Copies of the two sketches.

PREPARATION REQUIRED

Practise the sketches.

SKETCH

Reader 1: (Reading newspaper) That's terrible!
Reader 2: What is?
Reader 1: What happened to this girl.
Reader 2: What girl?

Reader 1: Kelly. Her name was Kelly.

Reader 2: What do you mean *was*?

Reader 1: She killed herself after being bullied.

Reader 2: That's terrible. What happened?

Reader 1: Some kids thought it was a good laugh to throw butter and eggs at her house.

Reader 2: Why did they pick on Kelly?

Reader 1: I don't know really. They were bored, she was an easy target and they thought it would be a good laugh.

Reader 2: I knew some kids who used to bully this boy in our road, just because he was a bit different from the rest of us.

Reader 1: Umm. I'm not surprised really, because it says here that according to the children's charity 'Kidscape', they get hundreds of calls every week from parents and children who say they are being bullied.

Reader 2: More should be done to help kids who are bullied.

Reader 1: Yes, I agree, but the trouble is that the children who are being bullied don't usually tell the right people about it, or if they do tell, nothing much is done to stop it.

TALK

Sadly, it is true that the people who are being bullied don't always feel that they can tell someone about it. There may be various reasons for this, but one reason can be that they think they will be bullied more if nothing is done about it or the bullies get away with it.

Bullying is something every school, every teacher and every parent needs to take seriously. It may all seem pretty harmless at first — just a bit of teasing or name-calling. But even that can be very upsetting, and if nothing is done about it things can get a lot worse. Some children say that they were bullied throughout their school career, and that can have disastrous effects. They may underachieve, lose sleep, find it difficult to make friends and end up being ill or unable to go to school because it is all too much for them. The next sketch shows what one bully did and how he finally got what he deserved.

BACKGROUND

(The scene is set in the head's study where the head-teacher is questioning the bully.)

Head: So, you thought you could get away with this kind of behaviour, did you?

Bully: It wasn't me. I was only hanging around there because I was bored and didn't have anything else to do. I didn't even touch that boy's PE kit.

Head: Right, well, we'll see about that. *(Picks up telephone and contacts secretary.)* Hello, yes. Could you send Philip in please? Thank you.

(Enter Philip.)

Head: Now Philip, don't be afraid. I just want you to tell me what happened yesterday behind the gym.

Philip: (Nervously) I was round by the gym at break-time. I was just eating my crisps and waiting for the bell to go before the PE lesson when *he* came round with a couple of his mates and started picking on me.

Head: What exactly do you mean — picking on you?

Philip: Well, he started kicking my bag and asking for some of my crisps. When I said, 'Get your own crisps' he got really nasty.

Head: What did he do? Did he call you names or was there more to it than that?

Philip: No, I mean yes. He did call me names. Said I was a wimp and things like that. Then he grabbed my bag and started chucking my PE kit about. Then his mates joined in and by the time the bell went, my stuff was covered in mud and I couldn't find my pencil case or my equipment.

Head: Has this kind of thing happened before?

Philip: Well, not exactly, but he's been on my back ever since I came to this school. I don't know why. I've never done anything to him.

Head: Thank you, Philip. *(Addressing bully)* What have you got to say about this, Sam?

Bully: He's making it all up. I never touched his bag or his precious crisps. Why would I? I had my own. Anyway, it wasn't me that took his bag or his PE stuff. I wouldn't touch it if you paid me.

Head: We'll see about that. *(Picks up phone again and asks secretary to send in the other witnesses.)* Now boys, I want you to tell me exactly what happened behind the gym at break yesterday. Did you have anything to do with taking Philip's PE kit and his bag?

Witness 1: I admit I was there, and I did see Philip's PE kit being thrown around. But I didn't touch it myself.

Witness 2: I saw it too, but I didn't have anything to do with taking Phil's bag. I did have his pencil case at one point, but that was only because I picked it up when it fell out and landed in the mud.

Head: So, if I'm to believe you two, it wasn't anything to do with either of you. If it wasn't anything to do with you, who was responsible? You had better tell me that right now as I'm about to phone both your parents and ask them to come up to the school to sort this out. Well? I'm waiting!

Witness 1: Please, don't tell my mum and dad. I didn't touch Philip's stuff. It was him *(pointing to bully)*. He's always getting us into trouble. Picking on smaller boys or annoying the girls. I'm fed up with taking the blame for things he keeps doing.

Head: You're quite sure about this? You're not saying it to get yourself off the hook? You admit you were there, so how do I know it wasn't you?

Witness 2: It wasn't him. He's telling the truth and so is Philip. I admit I was there, but neither of us started it and we didn't have anything to do with calling Philip names or taking his stuff. It was Sam who took the bag and it was Sam who threw his PE kit around and trampled it in the mud.

Head: (To bully) It seems to me that the evidence is stacked against you, Sam. Besides, I know it was you because the caretaker told me last night that he saw you bullying a boy behind the gym, but he didn't know who the boy was until he picked him out in assembly this morning. What have you got to say for yourself now?

Bully: OK. So it was me, but I didn't mean it to go so far. I was only out for a laugh and a bit of fun. He's got his PE kit back anyway, so I can't see it's such a big deal.

Head: We'll see what your parents have to say about that, Sam. I don't think they are going to be very happy about what you've done. It's not the first time you've been in this sort of trouble, is it?

Bully: No, Sir.

Head: As for you two *(addressing witnesses)*, you could have done something to stop what was happening and you certainly didn't have to just stand by and watch. I will be writing a letter home. Meanwhile, I think you owe Philip an apology, and I don't want to hear that you've been involved in anything like this again. Understand?

Witnesses: Yes, Sir. Sorry, Sir. Sorry, Philip.

Head: As for you Sam, you will not go back to class. You will be working on your own outside my office for the rest of today at least. The rest of you — back to class now!

REFLECTION/RESPONSE

Bullies are not popular people, although they have a few friends who think that it is a laugh to pick on other people who they may see as being weaker than themselves. As we have seen, bullying people can have very serious consequences, and in the end, bullies usually get what they deserve.

I hope none of you ever pick on people or bully others in any way, and if you're ever bullied yourself, I hope you will have the courage to recognise that bullies need to be stopped and that you will play your part in bringing them to justice.

TO THINK ABOUT

How do you think bullies should be punished?

18

THEME

Lost and Found

FOCUS

The Christian belief that no one is ever lost to God.

SUMMARY

This assembly is about losing things and finding things. The main story of the lost son shows how the father never stopped loving his son and never gave up hope of his lost son returning home.

RESOURCES

A selection of items from the school's lost property box.

PREPARATION REQUIRED

None.

TALK

What do you do when you lose something in school? *(Allow time for a few different answers.)* A lot of the things people lose in school end up in the lost property box. It's amazing what some people lose. *(Show a selection of some of the more interesting items from your school's lost property box.)* One lost property office in a large city had among their collection of lost goods, a selection of toys, buckets and spades, a child's bicycle, a box of kippers, two prams, several pairs of false teeth, walking sticks and a large number of umbrellas. How can anyone lose their false teeth?

Police stations often house collections of lost property and it is the most obvious place to go if you lose something. Tom decided to report his missing bicycle to the police. He had ridden it into town and left it for a brief time outside different shops while he went in to make his purchases. It had been there when he came out of the first two shops, but when he came out of the last shop it was nowhere to be seen. At first he thought some friends who worked in the nearby offices had hidden it for a joke, but they said they knew nothing about it. He went back and looked again, but still no sign of his bike. The only thing to do was report it to the police. It must have been stolen.

The police listened carefully to Tom's story about his missing bike and took down all the details. They were not surprised to hear the bike had gone missing. Recently there had been a few other similar cases. They said they would get onto it straight away and asked Tom if he would ride in the police car with them while they made a search of the local area. There was just a chance they would find the culprit and Tom would be able to identify the missing bike. Tom agreed — after all he would have to walk home or get the bus if his bike didn't turn up soon. The police car sped off down the main road, first one way, then the other. No sign of the bike. Then just as they were about to try another part of the town, Tom had this strange sinking feeling in the pit of his stomach. It suddenly began to dawn on him that he had not left his bike outside the shop at all. He remembered that he had left it outside another shop and walked to the last shop. Tom was feeling very uncomfortable now and wasn't sure whether or not to admit to his mistake. After all, it had been some time ago that he had left the bike there, so it might have disappeared by now anyway.

Finally, Tom owned up to his mistake. The policeman driving the car said he would take Tom back to the place where he now thought he had left his bike to see if it was there. As the shop came into view, they saw it, still standing by the pavement, just where Tom had left it! Fortunately for Tom, both the police officers saw the funny side of the incident and let Tom off with a warning about wasting valuable police time.

Jesus told three stories about lost things. The first one was about a woman who lost a coin. It fell on the floor of her home, but she just couldn't find it. She was quite poor and couldn't afford to lose it, so she lit a lamp and got out the sweeping brush to try to find the coin. She had to sweep the whole house, but when she did find it, she was so pleased that she asked all her neighbours round to celebrate with her!

The second story was about a sheep that wandered off and got lost. The shepherd went after it, searching everywhere until he found it.

The third story was about a lost boy. It was his own fault. He wanted to go off and have a good time, so he persuaded his father to give him his share of his inheritance, which he would normally have got when his father died. His older brother wasn't happy about being left to carry on with the work at home while his younger brother went off abroad to enjoy himself. The father loved his son very much and worried every day about him. He knew that there would be plenty of people waiting to help his son spend his money and he would soon be in problems if he just frittered it away.

And that was just what happened. The boy lived it up for a while, but soon his money was gone and so were his friends. He ended up having to take a job looking after pigs just to keep body and soul together. He got so desperate that he even tried eating the food he had to give to the pigs! His thoughts often turned to home now, and he wondered what kind of reception he would get if he went back.

Finally, he decided that he would swallow his pride, go back home and ask his father to take him on as a servant. At least he would have a roof over his head and food to eat. So, off he went. Eventually, as he neared his home, he saw someone running towards him. He couldn't believe it at first, but it was his father actually running down the road to meet him. He started to ask for his father's forgiveness and for the chance to work for him as a servant, but his father would have none of it. Instead, he called for water to be brought for the boy to wash in, gave him clean clothes to wear and put a ring on his finger. Whatever the boy had done, that was all in the past now. The father was just happy to have his lost son home again.

REFLECTION/RESPONSE

Jesus used these three stories to show the people listening that God is always very happy when people who have been away from him find their way back. The story of the lost son in particular paints a wonderful picture of a father's love. Despite everything the boy had done, the father still loved him and showed his love openly by running to meet the long-lost son and restoring him to his former position in his household. Jesus said that he was on a mission to find lost people and bring them home to Father God. This is why he had come into the world, he said, 'to seek and to save that which was lost'.

TO THINK ABOUT

In the story of the lost son, the boy's brother was not very happy about the way his father welcomed the boy back and treated him as though he had never been away. He boycotted the party his father threw for his brother and refused to join in the celebrations. Why do you think this was?

NOTES
See Luke 15.

19

Ready, Steady, Cook!

FOCUS

Making the most of what we've got.

SUMMARY

This assembly is about using the different talents and abilities we have to make something special of our lives. It uses the *Ready, Steady, Cook!* programme as a way in to the subject.

RESOURCES

Two bags of ingredients *(see below)*. Two contestants and two 'celebrity chefs'. A box labelled 'Ingredients to make a special person'. Some personal qualities written on slips of paper. One card with a red pepper on it and one with a green pepper to denote the red and green kitchens.

PREPARATION REQUIRED

The 'chefs' and contestants will need briefing on their roles.

TALK

Ask if anyone has seen the *Ready, Steady, Cook!* programme. Explain briefly how it works — two contestants bring a bag of ingredients for the two celebrity chefs to use as a basis for a wonderful meal for two people. They are not allowed to spend more than £5 on their ingredients. Once the two chefs have been introduced and placed in the green or red pepper kitchen, the contestants empty out the contents of their bags and the ingredients are examined. The chefs have to say how they are going to use the food brought in by their contestants and what kind of dishes they are going to make from it. They have twenty minutes to do the preparation and the cooking and to serve up the finished dishes. The audience then vote using their green or red pepper cards to show which team they think have come up with the best menu, considering the ingredients they were given.

Explain that you are going to put on your own version of *Ready, Steady, Cook!* this morning. Introduce your two chefs (these may be pupils or willing members of staff) who are going to play *Ready, Steady, Cook!* Assign them to the red or green kitchen, then invite your two contestants to bring out their bags of food. Explain that they only had £1 each to spend on their ingredients. Show the contents of each bag. One might have a tin of baked beans, one onion, an egg and a banana; the other contestant could have a potato, a small cabbage, a pot of fish paste, some mustard and an orange. Suggest that it will not be easy for the chefs to make much out of this strange mixture of ingredients. The chefs could then say what they plan to do with the goods, eg, make an onion, bean and banana omelette, and a jacket potato stuffed with fish paste and stir-fried cabbage, followed by an orange and mustard cocktail.

Suggest that the chefs and the two contestants go off and get on with their task, then continue on the following lines:

Of course, in the real programme, the contestants bring along a rather better set of ingredients from the ones brought in by the two contestants this morning. There is no way you can make a really tempting and tasty meal out of poor or mismatched ingredients. You need the right things to start with. However good a cook you may be, you can't make a great meal out of a tin of beans and an onion. You need the right ingredients to start with. As the saying goes: 'You can't make a silk purse out of a sow's ear.'

This principle can be applied to most things in life — not just cooking! For example, it would be very difficult to make a good job of decorating your room or putting together an exciting or interesting project on a certain topic if you haven't got the right materials to start with. In the same way, it is hard to make something of our lives if we don't have some 'good ingredients'. However bright or clever a person may be, they are not likely to be very successful at making friends if they are always talking about people behind their back, telling lies or boasting. What ingredients do you think a person needs to make a success of life? The following story shows how one boy used what he had to get what he needed.

A fourteen-year-old boy from New York needed a job for the summer holidays, so he scoured the local papers and adverts in the local shops for a suitable post. Eventually he saw an advert which read: 'Wanted: bright boy for light duties. Early start. Good wages.' It sounded perfect. He rang up to find out more and was told to report for an interview at 9 am the next morning. Keen to make a good impression, the boy arrived early for the interview, but to his dismay he found there were already another twenty boys sitting waiting for an interview. He realised that with twenty bright-looking boys in front of him, his chances of getting the job were slim. After sitting there for some time watching the other boys go in for their interviews, he had an idea. He got a piece of paper and wrote something on it. He then went over to the secretary's desk and very politely asked if she would pass this very important note on to her boss immediately. The secretary looked at the note and smiled. She said that she would and disappeared into the inner office where she laid the note down in front of her boss. He read it and laughed out loud. This is what it said:

Dear Sir

I am the twenty-first kid in line for this job. Don't do anything until you see me.

It was enough to get the boy the job. He had the initiative and resourcefulness to see how he might overcome the problem facing him, as well, no doubt, as the qualities needed to do the job successfully.

REFLECTION/RESPONSE

Resourcefulness and initiative are two important ingredients to take through life if we want to be successful. What other qualities or ingredients can you think of? *(Make a list of their responses on the OHP or flip-chart if time permits.)* Look at the list drawn up, then invite pupils to join together in thanking God for all the gifts and abilities they have. They may also like to ask for God's help in developing the many positive qualities included on the list. Alternatively, the different qualities may be written down in advance on slips of card or paper. As each one is read out, a pupil can be invited to come out and place that quality in a box marked: 'Ingredients to make a special person.'

TO THINK ABOUT
What qualities does the Bible highlight as being necessary to make a happy and successful person?

20

Masks

FOCUS

Accepting ourselves the way we are.

SUMMARY

This assembly is about 'wearing a mask' in an attempt to hide what we are or what we really feel. It challenges pupils to see themselves in a positive way as unique individuals, accepted and loved by God.

RESOURCES

Some animal masks.

PREPARATION REQUIRED

None.

TALK

(Get some volunteers to come to the front to put on the animal masks. In turn, each volunteer should then pretend to be that animal and try to take on its character, making the noise of their animal and mimicking its actions. When each volunteer has finished, go back and ask the rest of the pupils to comment on each one's por-

trayal of their animal and give their verdict on how convincing each one was. Thank the volunteers as they return to their seats.)

Leader: There are times in life when most of us like to put on a mask. Not a real one, like these animal masks, but a 'front' to cover up our true feelings or what we really are. Some people really find it difficult to accept themselves the way they are, so they try to be something or someone else.

Some of you may know the story of a goat who didn't like the way he was. He wanted to be powerful and important, like the lion. So he decided to try to be a lion. He went about roaring like a lion and eating lion's food. All the other animals thought it was quite bizarre and very funny. They could see that whatever the poor goat tried to do to be a lion, he never would be a lion because underneath he was a goat. Once a goat always a goat. There was no changing what he was.

Some people find it difficult to accept the way they look. They colour their hair and spend thousands of pounds on face-lifts and plastic surgery in an attempt to improve their appearance. They may succeed in changing their appearance, but their real problem may go deeper than that. It may be that they are not happy with the way they are.

Other people try to mask their true feelings by putting on a brave face or pretending that everything is OK when it isn't. They are unable to admit that something is wrong. The Beatles' song 'Eleanor Rigby' talks about 'all the lonely people'. Eleanor 'waits at the window wearing a face that she keeps in a jar by the door'. She hides her feelings of loneliness behind a mask so that nobody knows.

Some people hide behind a mask because they have a low self-esteem and feel that they are of little worth. They compare themselves with other people and think that in comparison they have nothing to offer. They may pretend that they feel good about themselves, but underneath that brash exterior they feel a failure. They cannot accept themselves as they are and see that they are equally as important and valuable as anyone else. They need to swap their 'nobody' mask for a 'somebody' one. They need to discover their true identity and build on what they have.

Rod Laver and Ken Rosewall, two Australian tennis players, emerged as great champions in the 1970s, yet as young players they did not seem to have the hallmarks of future champions. Rod was very slow-footed, but his coach nicknamed him 'Rocket'. Ken was very slim and spindly, so the coach named him 'Muscles'. They lived up to the self-image portrayed for them by their coach and became two of the greatest tennis players in the world. They didn't have to pretend to be great — they were great! The image we have of ourselves helps us to determine what we will become. If we have a defeated self-image, we will be defeated, but if we have a mental image of ourselves as we want to be and strive for it with all our heart, then, with God's help, we can be what we want to be.

Another 'sporting great', the runner Roger Bannister, believed that through running and his dedication to his sport he learned a lot about himself. He said that in sport one runs into situations that are too big to master. In real life one can dodge the issue and play hide and seek with reality, never facing the truth about ourselves, but in sport that's not possible. Sport leads to the most remarkable self-discovery of one's limitations as well as of one's ability. This moving towards the realisation of the best that is within everyone is, he says, 'the quest of a lifetime'.

It is time to take off the masks (as our volunteers

did earlier) and see ourselves as others see us. It is time to make the most of what we have and face up to the challenge to be the best that we can be.

REFLECTION/RESPONSE

Jesus told a wonderful story about someone who hid behind a mask of good works and generosity, when really he was fooling nobody, including God! The story is about a man who wanted to give something to a beggar. He couldn't do it quietly. So he sent his servant out to buy a trumpet, then he made the servant walk in front of him, blowing the trumpet as loud as he could. Everyone heard it, and word went round that a very rich man was going to give away some money to the poor. No doubt things got exaggerated a bit with people saying that they thought it would be a lot of money, probably thousands of pounds! There was plenty of noise anyway, so it must be something really big. A crowd gathered, waiting for the big event. The rich man singled out the beggar and called him forward. He then handed him a penny before going off with his servant and the trumpet. All that fuss about giving away a penny!

Jesus said that this was not the right way to do things. If we want to do a kind deed, we should do it quietly and without anyone knowing. This man was a member of a religious group called the Pharisees and Jesus had some harsh words for them. He called them hypocrites and a brood of vipers! What he meant by this was that they pretended to be something they were not. They acted as if they were so holy and so careful about fulfilling all God's laws on the outside, but they were not so virtuous on the inside. God saw what they really were. He could see behind the mask.

The story is told of a boy who came running out of school carrying a prize he had won. He was shouting, 'Look how clever I am!' His mother heard him and taught him something he would never forget. 'Cleverness that must be mentioned,' his mother said, 'does not exist.'

Christians believe that God sees behind our masks and accepts us as a person of worth and value just as we are. We do not have to earn God's love or try to be a different person. He sets us free to be ourselves — and to like it.

TO THINK ABOUT

Are you wearing a mask? If so, perhaps it's time to take off the mask and let people see you as you really are.

NOTES
Adapted from an original idea by David Hughes.

21

THEME

The Price is Right

FOCUS

The worth and value of every individual.

SUMMARY

This assembly highlights the worth of every person and encourages pupils to think about the difference between the way some people value others and the way God values people.

RESOURCES

OHT of objects for pupils to guess their price. These could be taken from a catalogue that will give you the prices. Four items and four price tickets. An OHT of the cartoon drawing of a baby (provided).

PREPARATION REQUIRED

The OHT, four objects for pricing and the four cards with the correct prices on them. Two pupils to read out the statements for reflection.

TALK

Who has watched the TV game show called *The Price is Right*? First, four suitably surprised contes-

tants are summoned to 'come on down' and take their places on the stage. Then the show's host, Bruce Forsyth, invites each of them in turn to guess the price of an item that will be given away to the person who makes the best guess. They then have the chance to go on to another game and win an even bigger prize and compete in the final 'show-case showdown'.

(Say that you are going to play your own version of The Price is Right now. Ask for volunteers to come on down and join you! If possible, have some sticky name badges ready to slap on the contestants. Line the four chosen pupils up behind a table or four desks, then invite them to put a price on the first item shown on the OHT. Reveal the correct price. The winner is the person who got nearest to the correct price without going over. The winner then plays the second game. This involves putting the four correct price cards on the four correct items. If they get them all right, they could be rewarded with a suitable 'prize'. Thank all four players.)

In this game, the contestants had to try to put the right value on each object. This isn't easy, especially when you consider that different shops may charge very different prices for the same items. People also place different values on different things. If, for example, the object is something you really want, then you may put a much higher value on it than someone else might do. People also put different values on people. Slavery is a terrible example of the lack of value some people put on other people's lives, making slaves of them or buying and selling them in the market place. They treated people as though they were objects without feelings and without the right to live their lives in the way they wanted to.

The slave trade was a dreadful thing. Slaves were often taken from their homeland and transported to other countries by sea in the most appalling conditions. Crammed together in the holds of the ships, many fell ill on the journey and even died on board the ship. When a ship carrying slaves came into port, people would keep clear of it, afraid that they might come into contact with the slaves. They knew that the slaves might be ill and carrying some disease.

In the seventeenth century, a man called Peter Claver lived in Cartagina, a port where many slave ships came. Unlike many people of that town, Peter did not run away or avoid the slave ships. On the contrary, he would go out to meet the ship and go down into the smelly holds where the slaves were held. The conditions there were shocking, but Peter did not let this stop him from doing what he could to help these poor people. He would take them water and food and clean up their wounds and tend their needs. He would even pay for the bodies of slaves who had died on the trip to be taken to shore and given a proper burial. Peter valued human life and saw these slaves on equal terms. In his eyes, every life was of value to God.

REFLECTION/RESPONSE
(Put up OHT of the cartoon of a baby.)
What would you say if I asked you to put a price or a value on this baby? How much is a baby worth? How much are we worth as human beings? It is a well-known fact that if you analysed people in chemical terms you would find that *none of us* are worth very much. Apparently our bodies contain:

> Enough:
> Fat for seven bars of soap
> Iron for one medium-sized nail
> Sugar for seven cups of tea
> Lime to whitewash one hen house.
> Enough:
> Phosphorous to tip 2,200 matches

Magnesium for one dose of salts
Potash to explode one toy crane
Sulphur to rid one dog of fleas
    And enough:
Water to fill six buckets!

If that's all an average human being is worth, then we wouldn't be worth much more than a week's pocket money! Most of us would consider that we have other qualities and facets to our nature than a few chemicals! What other qualities do we possess as human beings? What makes us the kind of people we are? Are some people worth more than others? *(Give pupils time to reflect on these questions.)*

According to the Bible, God considers every single person to be of great value as the following verses show *(these statements could be read out by pupils)*:

Reader 1: Genesis 1:27 says that God made us in his own image. This has to make us very special.

Reader 2: John 3:16 shows that God loved us so much that he was willing to pay a very high price for us. He sent his Son into the world to die on the cross so that anyone who believes in him can have everlasting life.

TO THINK ABOUT

How much value do you put on a human life? Do you treat everyone the same? What makes some people treat others very badly? Is this the right thing to do?

22

THEME

Every Second Counts

FOCUS

When time is running out.

SUMMARY

This assembly looks at the importance given to time and the ability to make every second count, especially when time is running out.

RESOURCES

A stop-watch, a whistle, three waste-paper bins and nine balls (borrowed from PE department). Six volunteers to play the game against the clock. Prizes for the winning pair. OHT of Ecclesiastes 3:1–8.

PREPARATION REQUIRED

None.

TALK

(Choose six pupils to come out and form three teams to play a game against the clock. Place the three bins at a suitable distance from the selected 'throwing' line. Three

*pupils stand behind the bins ready to collect the balls as
they are thrown. The other three pupils have to see how
many balls they can get in the bins in the time allowed.
It would be good to have three members of staff to count
how many balls make it into each bin. The pupils
behind the bins throw the balls back to their partners
whether or not they have entered the bin. Speed and
accuracy are paramount! Blow the whistle and start the
stop-watch as soon as everyone is in position.)*

Time is never more important or valuable than
when we have a limited supply of it. This has been
proved over and over again by people who have
been told that they only have a short time to live, or
there is a race against the clock to save a life or
achieve a certain task. The following true story
shows how every second can count when trapped in
a very dangerous situation:

Reader 1: Some of you may have heard of a man
called Captain Jacques Cousteau who was leader of
the French Navy's Underwater Research Group. One
day, he decided to take his team to a village in
France called Vaucluse to test out some new diving
equipment and try to discover the secret of the
fountain of Vaucluse. This wasn't a real fountain,
but a spring of water that fell from a cave pool into
the valley below.

Reader 2: Jacques and another diver, Didi Dumas,
put on their wet suits, strapped their air cylinders to
their backs and prepared their torches so that they
would be able to see in the deep, dark pool. They
dived in and were soon separated. As he went
deeper into the pool, Cousteau became uneasy. Didi
was nowhere to be seen. He began looking for him.
Then, 130 metres below the surface, Jacques saw
him. Didi was lying unconscious at the bottom of

the pool in a crumpled heap. His suit was beginning to fill with water.

Reader 1: Jacques knew that he hadn't got much time. He must get Didi to the surface as quickly as he could. He tried to lift Didi up and swim with him to the surface, but he was too heavy. He then tried clambering up the rocky sides of the pool, pulling Didi with him, but again he fell back exhausted.

Reader 2: In his panic, Jacques had forgotten that he had arranged with his crew that if they encountered any problems on the dive, he would tug on the rope that was attached to the divers in an attempt to get the crew's attention. He was feeling very tired now and he knew that there was not much time left. Didi might even be dead already.

Reader 1: Jacques tugged at the rope — no response. He tugged again. Still no response. A few minutes more and it would be too late. He tried again. At last! Someone on the surface had noticed his emergency signal and the rope was beginning to haul them up to the surface. It was only just in time. A few seconds more and it would have been all over for Didi and maybe Jacques too.

Reader 2: The team found out later that their compressor had been faulty and carbon monoxide gas had been poisoning their air supply. It could have been fatal. A few seconds more and it could all have ended in tragedy.

REFLECTION/RESPONSE

There are many references to time in the Bible. One of the best known passages about time is found in the book of Ecclesiastes, chapter 3. *(Put up OHT of verses 1–8.)* This passage expresses the belief that there is a right time for everything. *(Select certain verses to highlight as appropriate.)*

Time is a very valuable commodity, so why do so many people squander it? Some people seem to think that they will live for ever and fail to take full advantage of the time they have now to get on with things. Opportunities are wasted and jobs put off for another day. There are many sayings about time. Here are some of them:

Reader 1: 'Don't put off till tomorrow the things you can do today.'
Reader 2: 'No one is ever busier than they will be tomorrow.'
Reader 3: 'Lost time is never found again.'
Reader 4: 'Time should be valued like life itself.'
Reader 5: 'Do not boast of tomorrow, for you do not know what a day may bring forth.'

The apostle Paul, writing to the church at Ephesus, says, 'Be very careful, then, how you live — not as unwise, but as wise, making the most of every opportunity' (Ephesians 5:15–16). We need to make every second count.

Psalm 90:12 tells us that we should 'number our days aright, that we may gain a heart of wisdom'. This involves two calculations, one is to count the number of days you have already lived and the other sum is to calculate how many days we still have left. Not quite so easy! We cannot work that out, but we should think about the time we have and make up our minds to use the time we have wisely. We should aim to make 'every second count'.

TO THINK ABOUT
We all get 24 hours in a day — 1,440 minutes — to waste or to spend wisely. How are you spending yours? Are you making every second count?

112

23

Now is the Time

FOCUS

Using time wisely.

SUMMARY

This assembly is about valuing time and using it to
full advantage.

RESOURCES

A selection of objects used for measuring time — eg
an alarm clock, a travel clock, a stop-watch, an ordi-
nary watch, egg-timer, an advent candle with the
days marked on it, a picture of a sundial and a calendar.

PREPARATION REQUIRED

None.

TALK

We are all born into time and everything we do uses
up some of that time. We know this is true because
we have various ways of measuring time. Here are
some of the things we use to measure time *(show
objects)*. We measure the days and weeks by using a

113

calendar. We measure the hours and minutes in a day by using a clock or a watch. Years ago, before watches were invented, people measured time by the position of the sun in the sky or by using a sundial or they might have an hourglass, similar to this egg-timer. Time can also be measured by using a candle marked off at appropriate intervals *(like this advent candle which is burned down a little each day in the run-up to Christmas)*. Athletes measure the time it takes them to run a certain distance by using a stopwatch which breaks the time down into seconds and parts of a second.

Time is a very valuable thing. People realise this when they feel they may not have much of it left. Time seems to go by much more quickly as you get older. When you are young, time can seem to drag and it is easy to get bored. Young people often find it hard to wait for one thing to end before they are ready to move on to something else. But, whether we are young or old, there is still the same number of hours in a day and the same number of minutes in an hour and the same number of days in a week. They are ours to use wisely and to the full.

If we look back, we may remember many things that have happened in the past — a special birthday, a recent holiday or a visit to a theme park or somewhere exciting. We probably all have some memories from the past that are not so happy. You may remember when someone close to you was very ill or when you lost a pet for example. But whatever has happened in the past, there is usually nothing we can do about it now. We cannot go back and live that part of our life again, however much we may like to. In the same way, we cannot live in the future. There may be things we are looking forward to, but we cannot make them happen any quicker by thinking about them. We just have to learn to wait, because the only time we really have is now!

We need to live in the present and make the most of it rather than just wasting time or letting it pass us by. Today is the only time we have; yesterday is gone, tomorrow may never come. The only time we can be sure of is now.

This principle runs through the Bible. 2 Corinthians 6:2 says: 'I tell you, now is the time of God's favour, now is the day of salvation.' Ephesians 5:15–16 reiterates this truth with the statement: 'Be very careful... how you live — not as unwise but as wise, making the most of every opportunity, because the days are evil', or as the Berkley version puts it: 'Wise people... make the best possible use of their time.'

Napoleon said, 'Ask me for anything but time.'

Time is precious and even young people can find they haven't got the time for certain jobs because there are other more interesting or exciting things to do! I heard someone say recently that when they were a child, they thought their name was 'Hurry Up' because that was what her mother was always saying to her when she was young: 'Come on, hurry up!'

We all get 24 hours in each day — 1,440 minutes, to spend wisely or to squander, yet we can never bring back a single minute. The clock ticks on. The pages on the calendar are turned, never to be turned back again. What we have to do, we should do now. Time should not be wasted, it is far too valuable. Time should be valued like gold itself. There is a saying: 'Lost time is never found again.'

REFLECTION/RESPONSE

It has been said that 'time is God's gift to a fallen world'. What are you doing with your gift? Are you using it wisely? What did you do yesterday? Can you remember what you did last weekend? Most people are careful how they use their money, but some of us are not so careful about how we spend our time. There should be time for work and time to relax and enjoy being with our friends and family. Students who have sat down and tried to work out how they spent just one week of their life have found it a very interesting experience. They have soon realised just how much time they waste and they have decided that they should try to value time by using it more sensibly.

Nothing, then, is more valuable than time. As the writer of the book of Ecclesiastes has put it: 'There is a time for everything, and a season for every activity under heaven. A time to be born and a time to die... a time to plant and a time to uproot... a time to weep and a time to laugh... a time to mourn and a time to dance' (Ecclesiastes 3:1–8).

There is a right time for everything. Are you using your time wisely or are you wasting it?

TO THINK ABOUT

Accounting for how we spend our time is a scriptural principle. Hebrews 4:13 says that 'one day, everything will be uncovered and laid bare before the eyes of Him to whom we must give account'.

24

Confessions

FOCUS

The courage to admit mistakes.

SUMMARY

This is an assembly about making mistakes, getting it wrong, but having the courage to admit one's mistakes and taking steps to try to put things right.

RESOURCES

Optional — a picture of the Great Fire of London from a history textbook. Copies of the sketch.

PREPARATION REQUIRED

Pupils taking part in the sketch will need a practice.

TALK

John Farynor was baker to King Charles II. He had been the royal baker for five years with premises in Pudding Lane, London. One night, after a long weary day, he climbed the stairs to his bedroom above the bakery. He was soon asleep. What he hadn't realised was that a flame still flickered in one of the bread ovens which had not been damped down properly.

The flame grew and by 2 am on 2 September 1666 the fire in his bakery had sparked off one of the greatest fires in history — the Great Fire of London. *(Optional — show picture of an artist's impression of the Great Fire of London.)*

The fire burned for four days by which time 13,000 houses had been destroyed along with 87 churches. Remarkably only eight people died in the fire as most people had time to get out before the fire reached their homes. They grabbed what they could of their possessions and flooded into the streets filling the narrow roads to the area beyond the city where they set up camp. The damage to property was extensive. The fire blackened over 300 acres, and the famous Guildhall and the Royal Exchange were reduced to ashes. London smouldered for weeks afterwards.

Some good did come of baker Farynor's carelessness, however. The terrible slums that had covered much of the scorched area disappeared and the last traces of the Great Plague of 1665, which had claimed some 100,000 victims, were wiped out in a single week.

Hopefully none of us will ever be responsible for anything like this, but it is true that we do all make mistakes and sometimes we are careless or don't bother to put things right when we do something wrong. Sometimes people try to put the blame on someone else for something they have done wrong rather than admit to the mistake themselves. It can be very hard sometimes to confess or own up to the truth and face the consequences of one's actions.

In the TV programme called *Confessions*, people are confronted with something they did in the past and are expected to 'confess' to what they have done in front of the audience and all those watching the programme on TV. Sometimes they are brought face to face with the people they deceived or the whole saga is acted out to everyone's apparent enjoyment! A person's failure to own up to something they have done and confess to the truth can result in other people suffering or sharing the blame when it wasn't their fault. This sometimes happens in school. A whole class is sometimes punished because the 'culprit' fails to own up, as the following sketch shows:

SKETCH

(Action takes place in a classroom. The class is seated waiting for teacher to enter. In one corner of the room, a small group of pupils are crowded around a boy who is obviously upset and crying. The teacher arrives, the class stands and the pupils return to their places. Sam continues to be upset.)

Teacher: Good morning everyone.

Class: Good morning Mr Williams.

Teacher: What is the matter with you Sam? Why are you crying? *(Silence)* Well, I'm waiting! Somebody must know if Sam can't tell me himself.

Pupil 1: Please Sir, when we came into the classroom, someone took Sam's lunch-box and started passing it around. He's got it back now, but his crisps are missing and someone's taken a bite out of all his sandwiches.

Teacher: Is that so. I find it hard to believe that anyone in this class would do such a thing. I think the person involved had better own up. This has gone far enough.

Pupil 2: Please Sir, I don't know who did it, but I think it was only meant as a joke. I'm sure whoever did it, only did it for a laugh Sir.

Teacher: I dare say lad, but I don't happen to think it's very funny. Sam hasn't got anything to eat now and those responsible should have the courage to own up. So, I'll ask you all again. Who did it? I want to know! *(Silence)* Right. I'll give the person responsible until break to own up, otherwise everyone will stay behind and I'll continue to keep this class in at break-time for the rest of the week or until the person responsible owns up. Sam, you will come with me to the canteen later and you can get something from there for your lunch today. Now, let's get on with the lesson.

REFLECTION/RESPONSE

What do you think might have happened in this story? Do you think the person responsible owned up? What punishment should they get if they did? What should the teacher do if no one owns up and confesses to the 'crime'? People can get hurt or others may suffer if the culprit refuses to own up to their 'crime' or mistakes. If you have done something in the past that has hurt others or resulted in things going wrong, perhaps you should think about owning up to what you have done. Perhaps you can then do something to help put things right.

A PRAYER

Lord, help us to be truthful and honest. When we make mistakes or have done something that has hurt others, please give us the courage to admit to our mistakes. Help us not to be afraid to confess to the truth and able to accept the consequences. Amen.

25

<u>THEME</u>

A Powerful Book

FOCUS

The Bible.

SUMMARY

This is an assembly about the Bible. It looks at different ways in which people view the Bible and how some people are prepared to take risks to get the Bible to others.

RESOURCES

A Bible wrapped up ready for a game of 'pass the parcel' or several different translations and types of Bibles (eg a Gideon Bible, a presentation Bible — like the sort given at a christening or baptism — a Children's Bible, a family Bible, a pocket New Testament and/or an assortment of different translations).

PREPARATION REQUIRED

Doing up the parcel and arranging the music.

TALK

(Show your collection of Bibles and talk about the way they all look different although they are basically the same book. Explain any special use they may have or invite about six pupils to come to the front to play a game of pass the parcel. Explain that the parcel they are passing around contains something very powerful and that it could be very dangerous to be caught with it. When the music stops for the final time — ask the person holding it (or who had it last) to open it up. Build up the tension with comments like 'be careful — this could be very dangerous', 'I don't want anyone to get hurt', etc. When the Bible is revealed, continue with the talk.)

This may not look like a dangerous package to you, but many people have been put in prison or even killed for having a Bible like this in their possession or for preaching from it. Others have risked their freedom and their lives to smuggle Bibles into countries where it is a forbidden book or where people are unable to get hold of a copy for themselves.

Why is the Bible such a dangerous book? The answer may lie in the fact that Christians believe that the Bible is a very special book that has the power to change people and the way they look at life. Christians often call the Bible: 'the word of God' because they believe that the message and the ideas it contains come from God. It is like a guidebook or a manual that points people to God and has the power to change things. Because of this, some people are prepared to take personal risks to get the Bible to people who do not already know about it or have access to it.

One man who did just this is a man known to many simply as Brother Andrew. He was born in May 1928 and grew up in a devoutly Christian family in a small town in Holland. When he was eighteen Andrew joined the army, but at twenty years of age he was wounded while on active service in Indonesia. Andrew left the army and got a job in a chocolate factory. Finally, he accepted the challenge to take up full-time Christian work and eventually found himself involved in taking Christian literature and Bibles into communist countries. This was often dangerous work because you couldn't walk into countries like Russia, China, Albania and Hungary and start preaching about Christianity without risking imprisonment, extradition or worse. Carrying contraband Bibles past armed border guards as Andrew did was also full of danger, yet he took bags of Bibles into every country that was under communist regimes until the recent past.[1]

Still today, taking Bibles into countries like China is a hazardous task, but many Christians are still prepared to take risks in order to get the Scriptures into the hands of Chinese believers. Michael Lyne was a highly successful electrical contractor who established his own international electrical company, but at thirty-eight years of age, Michael decided that there were more important things in life than making money. He sold his shares for a mere £2,000 to his partner in the business which employed sixty staff, got rid of the Rolls Royce and moved to Cornwall with his young family. Not long after this, Michael became involved in taking copies of the Bible into China with the Asian Outreach mission. At fifty-seven, Michael is preparing for another trip to China. Even though Christianity is among the religions officially recognised by the state, people can still be put into prison for their faith. Pastor Lam, one of the Chinese Christian community's leading figures, has endured over twenty years forced labour in a coalmine because of his faith. People caught taking Bibles into China face having their Bibles confiscated and being ordered out of the country. The risks are still there.

Another Christian businessman found himself caught up in a Bible delivery mission to China when he was in the Far East on a business trip. He was not fully aware of the risks involved at the time, but he wanted to help the Christians there and so he agreed to take some Bibles with him. His story, 'Bibles to China' (told below in his own words) could be divided up and read by several pupils:

Some years ago I had planned a business trip to Hong Kong and China. Before departing the UK, I spoke to a missionary friend at my church who suggested that I might like to contact the Hong Kong Bible Society with regard to becoming a courier in taking Bibles to mainland China. I knew this might be somewhat dangerous and difficult, but while in Hong Kong I decided to contact them. After a very busy week, I did not have the opportunity to visit them. However, arrangements were made over the telephone for one of my drivers to collect what turned out to be a hold-all full of Bibles on the day that I was due to leave Hong Kong for Shanghai. I opened the bag and saw that there were books on the top. Other than that, I did not check any further.

I was making the trip to Shanghai with some other businessmen. We were travelling as an organised group. We checked in for the flight and I checked in the bag of Bibles along with my case. I knew in the back of my mind that there could be some danger if I was caught with the Bibles, but other than that I settled back into my seat on the aircraft and picked up a copy of the *China Post* to read. The headlines on the Hong Kong paper jumped out at me — 'Missionary expelled from China'. This was an article about an English priest who had allegedly been caught preaching in mainland China. He had also had all his possessions taken away. He was imprisoned for just over a week until pressure from the authorities secured his release. Naturally, I was very taken aback and nervous at the thought of being involved in smuggling Bibles into China, but what could I do? I was sitting on the aircraft and the Bibles were in the cargo hold. Should I tell my Chinese colleagues that I had this package or should I just keep quiet and hope for the best?

Fortunately, when we arrived at Shanghai the bags for the whole group were loaded onto a trolley and I decided to keep quiet, but my heart was pounding as we approached the customs check. The documentation that you have to complete going into China is quite formidable and I prayed hard that God would help me to get through. My prayers were answered and I duly delivered the Bibles a couple of days later to the rendezvous in Beijing.

REFLECTION/RESPONSE
Why do you think some countries have laws banning the preaching or teaching of Christianity?

TO THINK ABOUT
Do you think it is right for Christians to ignore laws or regulations about preaching or about taking Bibles and Christian literature into countries where this could be seen as illegal?

NOTES
1. Brother Andrew, *God's Smuggler* (Hodder and Stoughton: London, 1967).

26

Keep Off the Rocks!

FOCUS

Saving lives at sea.

SUMMARY

This assembly looks at how the lighthouse has played such an important role in keeping ships and their crews away from rocks and dangerous coastlines. It also tells the story of the Vicar of Morwenstow and the part he played in alerting his people to death on the rocks. Finally, there is a chance for pupils to think about and pray for the safety of ships and their crew.

RESOURCES

A child's bucket and spade and any other items available for a day at the beach such as a ring, frisby, beach-ball, etc. An OHT of the lighthouse picture provided.

PREPARATION REQUIRED

Two pupils for the sketch.

TALK

(This assembly opens with the following short sketch. Two pupils enter. Pupil 2 is dressed for the beach and is carrying a bucket and spade, etc. The following conversation ensues.)

Pupil 1: Hi! Where are you off to? Looks like you're all set for the beach!

Pupil 2: Yeah. Mum and Dad are taking us to Portland Bill for the day. I can't wait to get on the beach. I'm going to build the biggest sandcastle you've ever seen!

Pupil 1: Sandcastle? You'll be lucky!

Pupil 2: What do you mean?

Pupil 1: Hasn't anyone told you? There isn't any sand at Portland Bill.

Pupil 2: No sand? What do you mean no sand? Of course there's sand. It's the seaside isn't it?

Pupil 1: There's plenty of sea all right. But there isn't any beach and definitely no sand. Just a load of old rocks.

Pupil 2: Are you sure?

Pupil 1: Sure I'm sure. Been there lots of times myself.

Pupil 2: (Dropping bucket, spade and rest of the equipment.) In that case, I guess I won't be needing any of these then. I'll just have to settle for a swim.

Pupil 1: Swim? You must be joking! Swim?

Pupil 2: Yes. Swim! And what's so funny about that? You said there was plenty of water.

Pupil 1: Water, yes. But you can't swim in it!

Pupil 2: Why not?

Pupil 1: Much too dangerous. Even if you managed to get in the water, you'd soon be dashed against the rocks. No, sorry. You can't go swimming.

Pupil 2: Well, if I can't go on the beach and if I can't go in the water, what's the point of going to the seaside?

Pupil 1: You can always go up the lighthouse. That's really interesting.

Pupil 2: If I can't go on the beach and I can't even get in the water, how am I going to get in a boat to visit a lighthouse? Get real! What do you take me for? A complete idiot?

TALK CONTINUES

The first boy/girl is right of course. There is a lighthouse at Portland Bill and you don't have to get in a boat to see it. Some lighthouses are on the mainland and some are open to visitors at certain times. Perhaps someone has seen a real lighthouse or even been up one? This OHT *(put up picture of the lighthouse)* shows the lighthouse at Portland Bill, which is in Dorset. This lighthouse was built between 1903 and 1906 and it replaced an earlier building which now houses a bird observatory. The tower is 136 feet high and the light at the top is an electric one. It gives out a beam equivalent to 3,370,000 candle power or 3,000 watts. Ships up to 29 nautical miles away can see the light on a clear night and it flashes every 20 seconds. When it is foggy, the lighthouse sends out a 3.5 second blast every 30 seconds.

Can anyone tell me what a lighthouse is for? Yes, it is to warn ships of danger ahead. They need to keep well clear or they will be in real danger of being swept onto the rocks. In some parts of Britain the coastline is so dangerous that even today, with all their modern navigation systems, boats can still be swept onto the rocks in bad weather. For centuries, treacherous stretches of coastline around Hartland Point in North Devon were a graveyard for ships. Some say that the people here deliberately enticed ships onto the rocks because a shipwreck brought all kinds of booty and provisions for the poor people living there.

The Reverend Robert Stephen Hawker was a colourful character who lived in this area back in the nineteenth century. He was the vicar of Morwenstow in Cornwall, a small, isolated village which takes its name from the ninth-century Celtic saint Morwena. The ancient church, sheltered by wind-bent trees, is a ten-minute walk from the crumbling cliffs and rocky coves of Cornwall's rugged northern coast where the Reverend Hawker loved to go. From the cliff-top there is an unrivalled view of the Atlantic stretching from Lundy Island to Padstow Point. Overhead, gulls, choughs and other seabirds wheel and scream around the rocky crags.

The beach is inaccessible save at one point where a path has been cut into the sides of the steep gorse-covered slopes and the slate rocks to a bay below. A little way down this path, there is a hut made of driftwood and fragments of wrecked ships thrown onto this dangerous shore. The sides are formed from the curved ribs of vessels and the entrance ornamented with carved work from the figurehead of another ship. This hut was built by Robert Hawker and here he liked to sit, sheltered from the wind and rain, looking out over the wild sea, dreaming and composing poetry as he watched the ships scudding before the gale, often dangerously near the rocky cliffs.

From his pulpit, the Reverend Hawker vigorously condemned the plundering of wrecked ships. He knew that some of the people in Morwenstow were 'wreckers'. This meant that they deliberately set out to cause a ship to come too close to the coast so that they floundered and were dashed to pieces on the rocks. They did this by looking out from the cliffs for signs of ships passing on a stormy night. The crew would be looking for somewhere safe to shelter and see out the storm. Knowing this, the wreckers would set out lights on the cliffs that would be mistaken by the sailors for the lights designed to guide them to the harbour. Instead of being led to a safe place, the ships were steered onto the rocks. When they were aground, the wreckers would go down, board the vessel and take anything of value. Often, survivors would be murdered so they could not tell the magistrate what had happened.

Because of this work, many of the people around Morwenstow despised Robert and certainly kept well away from the church and his sermons calling on them to stop this awful practice.

REFLECTION/RESPONSE

Today, there are many people who still stand ready to go to the rescue of those who find themselves in difficulties and great danger from the sea and we would remember them. We think of those in the Royal Navy and people whose work takes them to sea. We think about the lighthouse-keepers and those who man the lifeboats and guard our coasts. We pray for the fishing fleets and the people who work in the docks and ports. We ask that you will keep them safe and help them in the work that they do. Amen.

THEME

Other People's Shoes

FOCUS

The ability to see things from another person's perspective.

SUMMARY

This assembly encourages pupils to consider a number of important issues from someone else's point of view. It asks them to put themselves 'in their shoes'.

RESOURCES

Several pairs of very different types and sizes of shoes — for example a pair of trainers, some smart 'dressy' shoes, a pair of very worn looking shoes, a pair of sandals, a pair of ballet or dance shoes and a pair of football boots and working boots.

PREPARATION REQUIRED

Hear the readers.

TALK

(Display the pairs of shoes where everyone can see them.)

You have probably heard people say, 'Try to put yourself in their shoes,' meaning 'try to see it from that person's point of view.' It can be hard to see things from another perspective, but if we want to live at peace and in harmony with our neighbours, here in school, at home and in the wider community, then we need to learn this lesson. For one thing we may not always be right and there will always be more than one way of looking at things. One of the reasons why we have disagreements with people is that we haven't really understood their situation or given them a chance to explain how they feel or why they think the way they do.

All these pairs of shoes are different *(point to shoes)*. They have been designed and made for very different purposes. Look at these, for example *(select two or three pairs and explain their particular use)*. It would be ridiculous to turn up for a football match in a pair of ballet shoes and it would be hopeless arriving for a day's work on a building site wearing a pair of evening/dress/party shoes. But each type of shoe here has a very real purpose and particular use. In the same way, the people who might wear these shoes are individuals too. They all have their particular points of view, their special interests and talents and their own unique way of looking at things and coping with life.

Listen to some situations and, if you can, put yourself in the shoes of each person as you hear each story. Try to imagine what they would be thinking in those circumstances and how they would be feeling. What would they want you to do? How would they want you to react? Think about this as you hear each person's story:

Reader 1: Marcia and her family came to this country to live some months ago. They have struggled to learn the language and settle into a very different way of life to the situation they came from in the country of their birth. They know very little about English ways and customs. Marcia talks with a heavy accent and has problems sometimes making herself understood. Because of this, some children laugh at her and make fun of her by imitating and exaggerating her accent. She is often left out of games and activities and is feeling very lonely and afraid. If you were Marcia, how would you feel? How would you want to be treated?

Reader 2: Paul's parents have struggled to bring up a large family on a small income. Because of this, Paul does not always have the 'right' clothes or the latest fashions to wear and feels particularly out of place and awkward at parties or school discos. He suspects that some children are talking about him and laughing behind his back at his appearance. He has now decided that it would be better not to go to any parties, discos or anything else where he might be shown up or made to feel 'out of place'. If you were in Paul's shoes, what would you want your friends and schoolmates to do and say?

Reader 3: Mr Morrison is leader of the new youth club. He works hard trying to plan an interesting programme suitable to the age group and aims of the club. But when he tries to explain something or organise an activity, some people talk out loud, clown around and throw paper or cans about. If you were in Mr Morrison's shoes, how would you feel and how would you like the members to act?

Reader 4: Young James thinks his older brother Tom is the best thing since sliced bread. He 'hero worships' him and wants to be just like him when he is his age. James often hangs around his brother and is becoming a bit of a nuisance, especially when Tom is trying to impress his new girlfriend. One day, Tom was talking to Mary in the park when who should pop up from behind the bench but Jimmie. Tom was so annoyed that he screamed at him and belted him one, almost knocking him to the ground. If you had been in young Jimmie's shoes, how would you have felt? How could Tom have better handled his brother?

(Thank the readers and continue:)

How did you feel about these different imaginary situations? Did you manage to 'put yourself in the other person's shoes'? It is often difficult to do, but try to imagine how you would want people to behave if it was you.

REFLECTION/RESPONSE

There is a verse in the Bible that is sometimes called 'The Golden Rule'. It is in Matthew 7:12. This is what it says (an OHT of the verse might be helpful): 'In everything, do to others what you would have them do to you, for this sums up the Law and the Prophets.'

The following extract from a poem about wearing other people's shoes expresses a similar thought:

Pray don't find fault with the man who limps,
Or stumbles along the road,
Unless you have worn the shoes he wears
Or struggled beneath his load.

There may be tacks in his shoes that hurt,
Though hidden away from view,
Or the burdens he bears, placed on your back,
Might cause you to stumble, too.

TO THINK ABOUT

This week, as you find yourself with other people who you might find 'difficult' in some way, try to 'put yourself in their shoes'. Ask yourself: If this were me, how would I want others to act?

NOTES
Virginia Whitman, *Programs that took with Teeners* (Moody Press: Chicago, Ill., 1961).

28

THEME
Wings

FOCUS

Wings as a symbol of protection, strength and eternal life.

SUMMARY

This assembly looks at some of the symbolism attached to 'wings' and uses a story to show how they can be a picture of protection. It also looks at some of the biblical references to 'wings' as a source of strength and protection. Finally, it tells the 'Waterbugs and Dragonflies' story sometimes used to help children understand what happens when they lose a pet or a loved one. This assembly will therefore need to be presented sensitively, especially if a pupil has lost a loved one or had a pet die recently.

RESOURCES

Some feathers.

PREPARATION REQUIRED

Two pupils to read the story.

TALK

Have you ever wished you could fly? Perhaps you have seen films or read books about people or beings who are able to fly — like *Superman* or *Fairytale* or a space or science fiction movie. Humans have long harboured a desire to fly and first took to the air in balloons and then began powered flight in airships and finally the modern aeroplane was developed. Planes today can have a wingspan of over 59 metres and, like Concord, cruise at a speed of 1,450 mph. Amazing!

Of course, nature has its own winged creatures that are just as amazing as a modern aircraft. These feathers *(show feathers)* come from a number of different 'feathered friends'. Birds are fascinating, beautiful and sometimes majestic and powerful creatures. They come in a variety of colours and sizes — from a tiny wren to a mighty eagle. Some birds teach their young to fly by pushing them out of the nest. The eagle does this when it thinks its offspring are ready to take to the skies. Then, if it sees the young bird plummeting towards the earth, it swoops down and catches the youngster on its own wings and carries it back to the safety of the nest.

Of course, not all birds can fly. The humble hen contents herself by scratching at the earth and laying her eggs within the confines of the barn or farmyard. She still has her wings though, and as the following story shows, although she may not fly, the humble hen can use her wings to protect her young.

Reader 1: A fire raged across Canada sweeping through forests, villages and farms. It devastated one particular farm in its path, leaving the burnt-out empty shells of many buildings and the farmhouse itself. When the heat had subsided and the

138

fire was completely out, the farmer started to count the cost of this tragedy. There was little left of what had been a busy, working farm and little hope of rebuilding what had been his livelihood.

Reader 2: Walking back across what had been the yard, the farmer noticed a pile of burnt feathers. He kicked at the charred heap and to his surprise, out ran a dozen or so baby chicks. The farmer realised that as the fire raged this mother hen must have called her chicks to her and gathered them under her wings for protection. There they remained until the fire had passed. The mother hen died in the heat of the flames, but the chicks survived the ordeal protected from the worst of the heat by their mother's wings.

TALK CONTINUES

There are many references in the Bible to winged creatures. Psalm 57:1 talks about taking refuge in the shadow of God's wings. In Exodus 19:4, God reminds the children of Israel how he brought them safely out of Egypt and carried them on eagle's wings. In Luke 13:34 there is another wonderful picture of the hen gathering her chicks under her wings for protection. The Gospel writer draws a picture of Jesus looking down on the city of Jerusalem lamenting the fact that he would have liked to have gathered the people of that city to himself like a hen gathers her chicks under her wings, but they would not come to him.

Other creatures that don't have feathers can fly. There are many beautiful species of butterfly, and if you are near a quiet pool of water you may even catch sight of a dragonfly. These are beautiful creatures that begin their lives in the bottom of the pond. Then, one day, they climb up the plants and out into the air above the pool, never to return. The water bug rests on the leaves on the surface of the pond and then wakes up to find that it has turned into a beautiful dragonfly with silver wings and a long tail. The warm sun soon dries its wings and it finds itself able to fly. It gradually grows accustomed to its new and exciting surroundings. But then it remembers that it had been a water bug, and when other bugs left the pool, the remaining ones were very sad and wanted to know where they were going. The dragonfly also remembers that it promised to return to its friends at the bottom of the pool to tell them what its new life was like. It tries to enter the pond, but it cannot penetrate the water's surface. No longer a water bug, but now a dragonfly, it cannot return to its old way of life.[1]

REFLECTION/RESPONSE

For some people, this story of how the water bug gets its wings and learns to fly above the pool in which it started out presents a beautiful picture of what happens when someone dies. When they leave the earth, everyone is very sad and cannot understand what is happening. They cannot know the beauty and wonder of life above the pond's surface until they experience it for themselves.

TO THINK ABOUT

Have you seen a dragonfly? If you do see one, perhaps it will remind you of this assembly and the fact that wings can give protection, offer security and lift us high above the circumstances and troubles that sometimes hold us back and stop us from appreciating the wonder and beauty of life.

NOTES
1. Doris Stickney, *Water Bugs and Dragonflies* (The Pilgrim Press, USA, 1982).

29

A Terrible Disease

FOCUS

Lack of desire or motivation for study and hard work.

SUMMARY

This assembly mentions some real diseases that affect humankind and then introduces pupils to a new disease that seems to be affecting many young people in the West — DON TSTU DYOSIS (ie Don't Study-osis). We look at ways of dealing with this problem and the results of letting it go unchecked!

RESOURCES

A number of cards with the names of several different, difficult-sounding diseases written on them. These must be large enough for everyone to see.

PREPARATION REQUIRED

Some pupils to come out and hold up the cards.

TALK

The human body is a wonderful thing. When it is working well, it can achieve all sorts of amazing

141

feats, like jumping over hurdles, weaving intricate patterns or designs, lifting heavy loads and performing delicate operations. We also have the sense of smell, taste and touch and we can enjoy the things we can see and hear. Of course, we also know that some people are either born without some of these abilities or they may lose them as a result of illness, disease or an accident. There are many terrible diseases that can strike a previously healthy person down and leave them incapacitated in some way.

(Invite the first pupil to come out and hold up the word TRACHOMA.)

For example, it is terrible to hear that in Adiyaman in Turkey, which many years ago had a population of 7,000, there were once 6,791 people who had lost their sight as a result of trachoma, an infectious disease of the eyes.

In America *(second card)*, around 3% of the population have GLAUCOMA, another disease of the eyes which, if left untreated or not caught in time, can cause blindness.

This disease, TRYPANOSOMIASIS, is caused by a microscopic single-celled organism called Trypanosoma. It is transmitted by the bites of tsetse flies and is found mainly in Africa. It can cause what is commonly referred to as 'sleeping sickness'.

There is just one more disease to mention today and it's called DON TSTU DYOSIS. This affects a lot of people in this country and can be found, often among young people, in most parts of the Western world. It often causes people difficulty in thinking or speaking. They may also have problems with their eyes, not being able to focus on the written page for any length of time, and some people find it hard to concentrate or remember things, especially when asked to respond to questions.

The shocking thing is that a lot of people here this morning are suffering from this disease. Quite a lot of young people suffer an attack of this disease when they reach their teenage years. If we turn the card over, we will see that the letters of the name of this disease have been misplaced. The spaces have been put in the wrong places. The correct name of this disease is really Don't Study-osis. Some of the symptoms of this disease are people asking questions like: 'Why should I study my lessons?' 'Why can't I watch TV instead of doing my homework?' These people have a bad case of Don't Study-osis.

One boy who suffered from a severe case of Don't Study-osis was Mick. Mick was a bit of a couch potato who would rather spend his evenings and weekends laid out on the couch or on his bed watching TV than putting in some study. He was quite a clever boy and especially good at science, but when there was an exciting science competition at school, Mick 'couldn't be bothered' to enter for it. When his friends asked him to help them with a project, he said he hadn't got time. Everything was just too much trouble for Mick. He could have done really well at school — all his teachers said so, but Mick never got the study habit. He had a bad case of Don't Study-osis.

Fortunately, Don't Study-osis is not an incurable disease. It can be overcome, but if left untreated it can cause people to under-achieve and leave them with feelings of apathy and a sense of failure.

There are many examples of the effect this disease has had on people in the past, although most of them have not been written down as they did not achieve anything of merit in the academic world anyway. It is easier to find examples of people who have worked and studied hard and realised their potential. Here are a few examples:

143

Reader 1: Elizabeth Blackwell wanted to be a doctor, but in 1845 that seemed an impossible dream. There were no women doctors. Encouraged by friends, she started to write round to all the doctors she knew to ask their advice. Everyone said that they thought the project was impossible, but she refused to give up. Then she was offered a teaching post where the headmistress's doctor husband would allow her to read his medical books in her free time. She agreed, and after several years of hard work and study, Elizabeth Blackwell obtained a place at a medical training school where in 1849 she won her doctor's degree and became the first woman doctor in the modern world.

Reader 2: Famous pianist Cyril Smith had many pupils who, according to Smith, thought that he was such a good pianist that he did not have to practise or work at his playing. This was not the case. Smith once made a recording of Rachmaninoff's third concerto. To most trained ears it sounded fine, but Smith was not convinced. He asked to hear a recording of the same work by the composer himself, and when he heard Rachmaninoff's recording, he asked the recording company not to release his own recording of the concerto. Instead, Smith spent the next three weeks practising the piece over and over again, six or seven hours every day, most of the time with his eyes closed so that he had to know every note and where to find it from memory. At the end of the three weeks, Smith went back to the recording studios and recorded the concerto again.

Reader 3: A famous artist, Frank O. Sainsbury, says that an artist's temperamental feeling may be his greatest asset, but that he would always be grateful for his disciplined training through which he had learnt to conquer his natural reluctance to work. He said that his motto was: 'Work for the inspiration: do not wait for it.' If you spend time waiting for inspiration, you may be too late.

REFLECTION/RESPONSE

We all have 24 hours in a day, and while some of it is taken up with sleeping, eating and going to school, we still have some time to use in whatever way we choose. Why not use some of it to defeat the Don't Study-osis bug?

TO THINK ABOUT

It is said that the hardest part of any task is the last 10%. How might that apply to your work and studies?

NOTES

D.M. Prescott, *Readings for the Senior Assembly* (Blandford Press: London, 1965).

30

Pets to the Rescue!

FOCUS

Pets who have saved people from dangerous, life-threatening situations.

SUMMARY

This assembly tells two true stories of dogs. One is a recent account of a dog called Boris who saved the life of his owner and the other story is about a dog called Bruce who saved a young boy from drowning in a muddy river bed. It invites pupils to think about the pleasure and devotion they can experience from a pet and gives opportunities for them to reflect on this.

RESOURCES

(Optional) Some tins of dog food or a packet of dog biscuits.

PREPARATION REQUIRED

None — unless you choose to let two pupils read the stories.

TALK

I know that some of you are not very keen on having breakfast before you come to school. This is not a good thing. You really should have something to eat in the morning, especially on a cold day. So, in case some of you are feeling hungry now, I've brought in a little something for you *(hold up dog food)*. Mmm, lovely meaty chunks and delicious tasty biscuits. Oh, you don't seem too keen on this either; not surprising really, I suppose, since this is actually for my/someone's dog. Mind you, the way some dogs behave you'd think they were humans — they seem to understand and be able to follow instructions a lot better than some people!

There are some fantastic stories about dogs and how they have helped or rescued people. Not so long ago there was a story about a dog who could detect when her owner was going to have an epileptic fit thirty minutes before it actually happened. By barking and nudging her mistress, she came to realise what her pet was trying to tell her. It didn't stop the attack happening, but she was able to take precautions so that she didn't risk getting hurt or injured. No one really knows how the dog is able to tell them an attack is close, but it could be that the dog senses something or is sensitive to some kind of chemical or physical change in her owner which even the owner is not able to detect.

Some dogs are very intelligent and can be taught to do lots of different things. Some are trained to sniff out drugs, others are trained as guide dogs and there are even dogs for the deaf who can do things like jump on their owner's bed when they hear the alarm clock go off and wake up their master or mistress. They can also be trained to respond to the telephone or the doorbell ringing.

There was a story in the papers a while ago about a marvellous dog called Boris. Boris is a pedigree

German pointer and very intelligent. His owner, Nicola, had a brain haemorrhage two years ago which has left her paralysed down one side. She normally has help in the home for certain things, like getting in and out of the bath, which is difficult and dangerous for Nicola. One day, Nicola decided to risk taking a bath without the usual help. It nearly cost her her life. As she got in the bath, she slipped and hit her head just where she had the haemorrhage. She was badly dazed and fell into the water. Her head was actually under the water and she was in danger of drowning. Fortunately, Boris, her faithful dog, sensed something was wrong. He got up on his back legs and placed his front paws on the edge of the bath. He then got hold of Nicola's arm in his mouth and pulled her up so that her head was clear of the water and wouldn't slip back in again. Boris was so gentle, that there wasn't even a mark on her arm. Nicola made a good recovery and is now full of praise for brave Boris's actions. She says that Boris keeps a constant eye on her and that she might well have drowned that day if it hadn't been for him.

Some of you may have heard another story about a brave and intelligent dog called Bruce. He was a friendly, gentle old crossbred Alsatian/Labrador who loved to play with children. He was often seen around with a four-year-old boy called Spencer who loved Bruce and had made a great friend of him. One day, about three months after the boy and the dog had met, Spencer did something which was not only unwise, it was also dangerous. Without telling his mother, he went down to the riverbank to play. It was some time before Spencer's mother realised that the boy was missing. She began a frantic search for him, but he was in none of the usual places he liked to go and no one had seen him. Then she thought of the river. She ran to the riverbank, but

148

still there was no sign of Spencer. Then she heard a faint cry for help. It was her son's voice. He was some way out from the riverbank, stuck in the deep mud with only his head and the top of one of his shoulders visible above the mud. It was then that Spencer's mum noticed another figure beside the boy. It was a dog. It was Bruce and he seemed to be lying on his side holding Spencer up by his shoulder so that he wouldn't sink below the muddy surface. Help began to arrive and soon the rescuers reached the spot where Spencer and the dog lay. Spencer was taken home and cleaned up and soon seemed to be no worse for his ordeal. It was clear that Bruce had saved Spencer's life. The dog must have held on to the boy for some time, but he must have done so without using his teeth, because there were no teeth marks on Spencer's body, just a red mark where Bruce had held him fast.

REFLECTION/RESPONSE

In a moment of quiet, you might like to think about the stories you have heard today and some of you might like to thank God for your pets or for pets like Boris and Bruce who have been such faithful companions. You may have had an experience yourself of where your pet has helped you in some way or you may know a true story about a pet who saved someone's life. Certainly, we all know about the work guide dogs and police dogs do and we can be thankful for their devotion to duty and wonderful service.

TO THINK ABOUT

What kind of award do you think brave pets like Boris might receive?

NOTES

Daily Mail, Friday 22 May 1998, p. 35.

31

THEME

St Jerome and the Lion

FOCUS
> Trust.

SUMMARY
> This assembly tells the story of St Jerome and the lion. It shows how quick people can be to jump to the wrong conclusions about someone.

RESOURCES
> OHT of St Jerome's emblem of a red cross on a silver field.

PREPARATION REQUIRED
> None.

TALK
> *(Put up OHT of the emblem of St Jerome.)*
> There are many different emblems or symbols that are attached to important people in the history of Christianity and the Church. This OHT shows a very simple emblem of a man who played an impor-

tant role in Church history — a man known now as St Jerome. He lived about three hundred years after Jesus and is remembered mainly for his work on the Bible. He translated it into Latin, and the Vulgate edition of the Bible, as it became known, has been used through the centuries in particular by the Roman Catholic Church. Of course, in Jerome's time, Latin was widely used and his work on the Bible meant that many more people were able to read and study it. Translating the Bible into Latin may not seem very exciting work to you, but there is another story about Jerome that you might find interesting. It is the story about Jerome and the lion.

After becoming a Christian, Jerome decided he would like to live in Bethlehem because that was where Jesus was born. He lived the simple life of a monk, working on his translation of the Bible and carrying out his duties in the monastery alongside the other monks.

Then, one day, a huge lion appeared in the monastery. The other monks fled in terror, but, according to the story, Jerome remained where he was. He noticed the lion was limping. He went forward to welcome the lion to the monastery and offered to tend its wounded paw. The lion was very grateful for the monk's gentle handling of his wound and instead of running back into the forest when his wound was better, he decided to stay and do some work for this kind man.

The lion soon got a job. It was his responsibility to accompany an ass which was sent out every day from the monastery to collect wood. The lion had the job of looking after the ass and seeing that she came home safely each evening. The lion and the ass soon became firm friends. Then, one day, a terrible thing happened. The sun was very hot and the lion got very tired, so he lay down and closed his eyes and was soon asleep. As the lion slept, some merchants happened to come that way. They saw the ass and walked off with it. When the lion woke up and saw that the ass was gone, he began to roar as only lions can. The merchants heard the lion's roars and they made off even faster. The ass it seemed had gone for good. What could the lion do now? He was afraid to go back to the monastery without his charge. What would the monks think? He had lost the friend he was supposed to be looking after. The lion laid down sadly outside the walls of the monastery. When the monks looked out and saw him, they immediately jumped to the wrong conclusion. They thought the lion had returned to its old ways and had eaten the ass. Jerome was the only one who still trusted the lion and believed that it had all been some kind of terrible mistake.

The monks refused to give the lion any food. They said that it could go and eat what was left of the poor ass. Then they made the lion go and fetch wood for the fires each day, just as the ass had done. The lion carried out the task very meekly and he never forgot his old friend the ass.

One day, when the lion had some time to spare, he decided to comb the district to see if he could find the ass. After some time, he came across a caravan of camels and merchants who were passing that way. He watched as they came closer, and to his great delight, there right in front of the camels, was his old companion. He was so delighted to see the ass that he let out a loud roar that sent the merchants scurrying into the forest. The lion went to greet the ass and led her and the camels back to the monastery.

The monks could hardly believe their eyes when they saw the lion approaching with the ass and twelve camels in tow! The merchants saw where their animals had been taken and soon came to the monastery to try to get their camels back. They fell on their knees before Jerome and asked him to for-give them for taking the ass in the first place. Jerome treated them with great kindness and said that they could take back what was theirs but that they should not touch what was not their own. The mer-chants were thankful and gave Jerome a present of some oil. They promised that each year they would send more oil as a sign of their gratitude.

After this, the lion and the ass became closer companions than ever before. They worked happily together serving Jerome and the monks at the monastery in Bethlehem.

If you are ever fortunate enough to go to Israel and see the town of Bethlehem for yourself, you will find that St Jerome is not forgotten by the monks who still live and work there. Close to the church that marks the place where it is believed the baby Jesus was born, there is a statue of St Jerome. A famous painting of St Jerome was also done. It shows him at work in his study with a huge lion beside him, lying like a dog asleep at his feet.

REFLECTION/RESPONSE

There is a saying you might have heard that a leop-ard never changes his spots. People mean by this that a leopard will always be a leopard and do 'leop-ardy' things whatever happens to it. In the same way, a person will always be the same kind of per-son they have always been — ie once a thief always a thief, etc.

The story of St Jerome and the lion shows us that it is possible for people to change for the better. Jerome still believed in the lion and thought of him as a trusted companion even when the evidence may have pointed to the lion going back to its old fierce habits.

Most of us have had times when it has looked as though a person we trusted has let us down, but we

154

should not jump to conclusions. It could be that things are not quite as they appear. We should always give people the benefit of the doubt and a chance to prove their innocence.

TO THINK ABOUT

Have you ever betrayed the trust of someone who has helped you?

32

Under the Influence

FOCUS

How others influence our lives.

SUMMARY

This assembly tells the story of Nick the Greek and shows how he came under the influence of various people who had an impact upon his life, some for the better, some for the worse. It asks pupils to think about the people who influence them and how they influence others.

RESOURCES

Pupils to read the story.

PREPARATION REQUIRED

Hear the readers.

TALK

The story of Nick the Greek.

Reader 1: Nick Pirovolos was born on the Greek island of Chios. He had a wonderful mother, but his father was always getting drunk and beating up his wife and the children. Most of his money went on drink and gambling, so the whole family had to work to earn enough money to feed and clothe themselves. They cleaned the church and attended the services there. Nick used to think that when he grew up he would like to be a priest.

Things got so bad in his family that his father and mother split up and his mother decided to try to take the rest of the family to join her eldest son in America. She didn't know that at the same time her husband was also applying to emigrate to the USA. When she realised that he was planning to come too, she broke down and cried. She could not face the idea of having him back in her home, even though he said he had changed his ways, but eventually she took him back and gave him another chance. Nick was excited about his new life in America. He thought it was a land of opportunity and he had dreams about becoming a millionaire.

Reader 2: The family went first to Michigan where the eldest son had a restaurant. He rented a house for them and they helped him in the restaurant, but soon they were on the move again, this time to Cleveland.

Things did not go well. Nick's father started spending his money on drinking and gambling again and then the beatings started once more. Nick did not have a good time at school either. He was struggling to learn the language and some of the pupils picked fights with him and he often went home with his clothes torn. He felt the teachers did not understand him either. His brother said they should stand up to the other kids, so they went home and got knives and meat cleavers which they

157

hid under their clothes. Then they went back to the school and attacked the children who had made fun of them. Although no one was seriously hurt, the boys succeeded in terrorising everyone and nobody was strong enough to stand against them after that.

Things went from bad to worse for Nick. He got a gang of boys around him who followed him into a life of petty crime, breaking into buildings and stealing money even from the churches, taking the 'poor box' which held money given to help the poorest people in the neighbourhood.

Reader 3: Things at home got so bad that his mum and dad split up again and were finally divorced, and Nick was sent to a special school. He began to settle down there with the help of a teacher called Mrs Flanders. Nick liked her and felt that she understood him. Then, sadly, Mrs Flanders became very ill and died; once more Nick went back to his old ways.

He was finally expelled from school for fighting. He continued with his life of crime, stealing cars and breaking them up to sell the parts. He made quite a lot of money this way, but then his mother found out what he was doing and Nick ran away from home. His brother was now in prison and Nick was afraid that he would end up in the same way. He tried to do something about his life and succeeded eventually in getting a job in some stables in West Virginia, but that didn't last long. He moved on to Akron where he was invited to a church service. The preacher showed him a lot of kindness and invited him to his home to meet his family, but Nick was restless and moved back to Cleveland. He tried to pick up the threads of his old life there and even went back with his ex-girlfriend. Together they set out for the open road. They got to Atlanta and Nick found a job there in a dog-food factory, but this didn't last long and Nick took up fortune-telling! He called himself 'The Devil's Son in Law'. Finally, after a bout of gambling in Florida, Nick ended up back in Cleveland.

Reader 4: In Cleveland Nick fell back into a life of crime. He did several robberies and finally he was caught and sent to prison. While in the prison hospital he met a man who had a big influence on him. This man was a Christian and he spent many hours sharing his faith with Nick. Nick realised that he needed to know God's love and forgiveness too, and eventually he became a Christian. This is not the end of the story though. After this Nick found himself in a cell on death row because there was no other available cell in the prison. He had a lot of time to himself there, but a man called Ernie Lavato, who was prison chaplain, gave him a Bible to read and Nick spent many hours studying it and praying.

He also met some other prisoners who were Christians and they encouraged Nick to share his faith through preaching. Nick was now trying to get parole from prison, but his attempt failed. All was not lost, however, because while he was still in prison he met Dottie. She visited the prison with a group of other Christians engaged in this kind of prison work. Nick and Dottie were married and Nick got his release.

Nick never went back to his old ways again. He started a prison ministry, visiting inmates and sharing his faith with them. His faith had changed his life and he wanted to share what he had found with others, like himself, who needed to hear that someone cared about them and that they could find love and forgiveness for themselves.[1]

REFLECTION/RESPONSE
From his earliest years, Nick found that life can be very hard and that one needs the help, encourage-

ment and understanding of others to face up to and cope with the challenges and difficulties life can bring. He soon discovered that different people have an influence on us and on the way we respond to things. Nick's father's bad habits made his home life very difficult at times and the way some of the other pupils treated him and his brother when he arrived in America also had an adverse effect on his life. There were people who had a good influence on him though, like his mum, his teacher Mrs Flanders, the prison chaplain Ernie Lavato and his wife Dottie.

Perhaps there is a lesson for all of us here. The people around us and the people we meet in our everyday lives influence us all to some degree. The people we choose as our friends also influence us. We can have an influence, for good or bad, on others. Nick finally got his life together by listening to people who had his best interests at heart. Who are you allowing to influence your life? Is it the people you know you can rely on to have your best interests at heart?

TO THINK ABOUT

What kind of influence are you having on your friends or younger members of your family? Do you really have their best interests at heart?

NOTES
1. Nick Pirovolos, *Too Soon to Die* (Kingsway; Eastbourne, 1982).

33

The Parable of the Three Balloons

FOCUS

Three different approaches to life and wealth.

SUMMARY

This assembly uses three balloons to illustrate three people's very different attitudes towards money and life itself. It shows how self-centred some people can be and how money can play an over-important role in their life. It also shows how a more balanced view can lead to a better quality of life and a more successful outcome.

RESOURCES

Three differently coloured balloons and three pupils (or teachers) to blow them up and help illustrate the story. A black felt pen for each pupil.

PREPARATION REQUIRED

A run through with the balloon blowers.

TALK

(Begin by explaining that three pupils (or teachers) will be helping you with the assembly today. They join you at the front ready to inflate their own balloon. As you mention each name the appropriate pupil adds their first puff of air into the balloon.)

Once upon a time there were three friends — Sid *(pause)*, Fred *(pause)* and Dave. *(Pupils draw a simple face onto their balloon as you speak about each character.)*

Sid: Sid grew up in the city and he became a very successful businessman. By the time he was twenty-five he had his own company and his own Ferrari *(blow the balloon up a bit more)*. Sid didn't come from a rich family, but he thought that making money was the best thing in life. If he could make a bit extra on a deal by bending the rules a bit, he would *(pupil puts more air into the balloon)*. Sid's main aim in life was to be a millionaire by the time he was thirty, and he wasn't too fussy how he did it. He didn't mind treading on a few toes as long as he pulled off the deal *(more air)*. In fact, people said that they thought all Sid cared about was himself — and making money *(another puff into the balloon)*. When he was thirty, Sid achieved his lifetime goal. It was official. He was a millionaire *(more puffs)*. So he decided to retire and put all his money into stocks and shares. He did well for a while, adding more and more money to his already bulging bank balance, until *(pupil keeps putting air into the balloon until it bursts — it can be helped by the use of a pin at the right moment)* the stock-market crashed and Sid lost it all.

Fred: Now Fred was very different from Sid. He liked money and he had a good job and a good salary *(start inflating the balloon)*. But Fred liked spending money too. He would earn a bit *(puff into balloon)*

162

and spend a bit *(let air out)* earn some more *(add more air)* and spend it *(let some air out)*. Fred was a bit of a spendthrift. He liked earning lots of money *(add more air)* and worked a lot of overtime to get more *(add more air)*. Fred never gave much away, he just kept spending it on himself. First there was the holiday *(let some air out)*, then he met Samantha and bought a new wardrobe of clothes to impress her *(let more out)* and finally he blew the lot on a new car *(let all the air out)*. Then Fred lost his job and ended up on the 'dole'. He had nothing.

Dave: Dave was different. He had a good job which was well paid *(start inflating balloon)* and he liked to have a good time *(let a bit of air out)* but he was sensible about the way he handled his money. When he got his monthly pay cheque *(add air)* he would pay his bills *(let some air out)* and put some aside for a rainy day *(add air)*. Dave thought about the future and opened a savings account which was growing nicely *(add more air)*. He was not a selfish man either. He cared about the poor and when he saw the appeal on TV for the starving people in the Sudan, he wrote out a cheque and sent it off *(let air out)*. He gave money regularly to his favourite charities and kept aside 10% of his salary to give to the church. His best friends knew Dave was a generous man and yet he always seemed to have money when he needed it. Money came in *(add air)* and money went out *(let some air out, but keep some air in the balloon)*. They were puzzled. 'How come you give so much away, but you always seem to have all the money you need?' they asked him. 'It's like this,' Dave said. 'I keep shovelling it into God's bin *(let a little air out)* and God keeps shovelling it into my bin *(put more air back in)*. The only difference is, God's got a bigger shovel!'

REFLECTION/RESPONSE

The moral of this story is clear. People who put their trust in money stand the risk of losing all they have — like Sid did. Others, like Fred, may enjoy spending the money they get, but they have nothing else to fall back on. Dave, on the other hand, used his money wisely. He paid his bills, enjoyed life to the full and still had the time and the money to fulfil his responsibilities to others and to God.

Many people use their money wisely like Dave. They pay their way in life, help others and set aside 10% of all they earn to give to God. They believe that by doing this willingly, they are pleasing God and laying up treasure in heaven. Like Dave, they believe that you can never out-give God.

TO THINK ABOUT

How are you using the money you get? Do you 'blow the lot' the minute you get it, or do you spend some time thinking about what you should do with it?

34

That's Amazing!

FOCUS

Incidents and events that take some believing.

SUMMARY

This assembly looks at some amazing modern-day stories that tell how 'the impossible' happened. It concludes with a story from the Bible that is equally amazing. Finally, it asks pupils if they can think the unthinkable and believe the unbelievable.

RESOURCES

None.

PREPARATION REQUIRED

None.

TALK

Have you seen the TV series *One in a Million*? If you have, you will know that it is about people who had an amazing escape or uncanny experience of some sort that almost defies belief. Some of the stories are truly amazing!

There was a story about a fully laden jumbo jet

that was flying between Malaysia and Australia. Most of the passengers were returning home from a holiday when the pilot found himself in a terrifying situation. There was trouble with the aircraft's engines. One suddenly stopped. This was no disaster in itself. The plane was still perfectly flyable and there was no immediate panic. Then a second engine stopped. This was more serious. It would be difficult now to control the plane properly, but the pilot and crew were trained for this kind of emergency and they were still confident they could cope and the passengers would be safe. Then the 'impossible' happened. The remaining two engines stopped. Total engine failure! This was unbelievable. No emergency training had prepared the pilot or the crew for this. The pilot kept his cool, but he was now flying the biggest glider in the world!

The plane fell 25,000 feet in a matter of minutes. The passengers soon realised that something was very wrong. The crew told them the situation and they began to prepare themselves as best they could for the inevitable. Unless the captain could get the engines to start up again, they would crash. The pilot struggled with the controls and tried desperately to restart the engines. One suddenly fired into action. That was a start! He knew there were mountains ahead, however, and one engine would not be sufficient to lift the plane over them. He tried again. A second engine came to life! Now they were in with a chance. Amazingly, all four engines came back on and the pilot was able to land safely in Jakarta. For the passengers and the crew, it seemed nothing short of a miracle. As the plane touched down, a great shout went up from the grateful passengers. The pilot's cool head and brave action had averted a major tragedy. They were safe.

Another story which was just as amazing in a different way, involved a man called Kevin Fisher and a girl named Tracy Watkins and her boyfriend. Kevin had just reached home one night and was getting out of his car when he heard an almighty crash at the end of the road. He realised immediately that there had been an accident and it sounded serious. Kevin rushed to the spot and found the couple dazed and injured. He saw sparks coming from the car and knew that he would have to act quickly if he were to get them out safely. Without any thought for his own safety, Kevin dragged the couple from the car and they were taken to hospital where they made a full recovery.

Six years later, Kevin and a friend were driving home from a night out when a car came up behind them. Kevin watched in amazement as the car went off the road and into the ditch. It burst into flames. They went to help. Both the passengers were injured, but the girl was trying to explain to her rescuers that the car could blow up at any moment because of the peroxide in the boot — she was a hairdresser and used this in her work. Kevin worked quickly to pull the couple from the car before the explosion came. Later, Kevin learned the name of the hospital the couple had been taken to from a newspaper report of the accident. He decided to go and visit them. When he got to the hospital he had a surprise. The young man, Richard, thought he recognised Kevin. It turned out that Kevin was the man who had rescued the same couple from their car six years earlier. Tracy believes that Kevin must be her guardian angel. What do you think?

A third story was about a man who decided to fulfil his ambition to make a parachute jump. He went to his local centre and booked a lesson. On the day of the jump, conditions looked good. With his instructors, Dave prepared for his first jump. It was awesome! At 5,000 feet, he gave his instructor the thumbs up, but then things began to go wrong.

First, as he pulled the ripcord to open his main chute, part of the rigging got trapped and he began to drift badly off course. His instructor had told him that there were five main hazards to look out for in parachute jumping. One was trees, another was roads, another was buildings, another was water and the last was electricity cables.

As Dave looked down, he saw four of the five things he had been warned about coming towards him very quickly. He decided to try to do something about it and change course. In his panic, he ejected the main chute and his reserve chute did not have time to open fully now. Dave was hurtling towards the ground at a speed of about 100 miles per hour. By this time, his instructors were back on the ground. They saw what had happened and watched in horror as Dave disappeared from view and into the trees. They raced to the spot, sure in their own minds that there was no way Dave could have survived such a fall. As they reached the spot, they saw Dave walking towards them. What had happened? How could he possibly have survived? It seems that the reserve chute had started to inflate as Dave reached the trees. This slowed him up a little. The trees themselves also cushioned his fall, and in Dave's own words he landed standing up! He walked away unhurt. Amazing![1]

REFLECTION/RESPONSE

All these stories are amazing and almost defy belief, but then, as they say, fact can be stranger than fiction. There are many stories in the Bible that may seem equally unbelievable when you read them. Take for example the story about the prophet Elisha. He was an incredible character who had an amazing belief in God and his power to do anything. One day, he heard about a widow who was in danger of losing both her sons because she could not pay her bills. Her creditors were at the door demanding payment. If she didn't pay up, they said they would take both her sons away and make them their slaves. Elisha asked the woman what she had in the house. She said all she had was a drop of olive oil. The prophet told her to collect up all the pots she could from her own home and from all the neighbours. Then she was to go inside, shut the door and start pouring the oil she had into the pots.

Amazingly, as she poured, the oil kept coming. It filled all the pots she had and when the last was full, the oil stopped flowing. Elisha told the woman to sell the oil and use the money to pay her debts and get what she needed.[2]

TO THINK ABOUT

If you like amazing stories, try reading some of the Gospel accounts about the miracles Jesus performed. They are truly amazing!

NOTES
1. ITV programme, *One in a Million*, usually transmitted Sundays, 7 pm.
2. Adapted from 2 Kings 4:1–7.

35

Recognising Our Faults

FOCUS

Seeing ourselves as others see us.

SUMMARY

This is an assembly about recognising that we all have faults and that we all make mistakes. It also looks at how we might try to put things right.

RESOURCES

Copies of the sayings and five pupils to read them out. Two pupils to read the short stories.

PREPARED REQUIRED

Hear the readers.

TALK

There is an old Greek legend about a camel who was part of a camel caravan. Day after day, these camels walked in a line, one behind the other. As they plodded through the desert, one camel became very amused by the sight of the camel walking in front of her. It had a strange hump on its back. The sight of it made her laugh, she thought she had never seen anything quite so funny. Of course, being unable to turn round in the camel train and never having stood in front of a mirror where she could see her reflection, she didn't realise that she too had a hump on her back, just like the poor creature walking ahead of her.

The Greeks say that some people are like this camel. They look at each other's humps or faults, but never see their own. It is much easier to see the faults in someone else than to see our own faults, isn't it? There are many well-known sayings about seeing other people's faults more easily than recognising or admitting to having faults of our own. Here are a few of them.

(Pupils walk on one at a time and read out their saying. Once they have read their statement they walk off.)

Reader 1: Nothing is easier than fault finding; no talent, no self-denial, no brains, no character are required to set up in the grumbling business. (Robert West)

Reader 2: Think of your own faults the first part of the night when you are awake, and the faults of others the latter part of the night when you are asleep. (Chinese Proverb)

Reader 3: She is generous to a fault — her own. (Arthur Baer)

Reader 4: All of us can live happily with our own faults, but living with the faults of others is almost impossible. (Anon)

171

Reader 5: Why do you look at the speck of sawdust in your brother's eye and pay no attention to the plank in your own eye? (Jesus, Matthew 7:3)

In a youth group meeting, the leader asked his group of teenagers to come up with a list of common faults found in people of their own age. Here are some of the things they came up with *(put list up on an OHT)*:

- Talking about people behind their backs.
- Thinking they know everything.
- Showing off.
- Boasting about what they've got.
- Making fun of people.
- Blaming others for things they have done themselves.
- Copying other people's work and making out they have done it themselves.
- Lying in order to get out of trouble.
- Bullying people who can't stand up for themselves.

No doubt you could think of a lot more things, but if you just look at this list, you might be able to see things which you dislike about other people you know. You might also be able to see something there that you know you are guilty of doing yourself.

Here are two short stories about people who had very annoying habits. The first one is about a person who couldn't stop talking about himself and how marvellous he was.

STORY 1

A young actor was on his first date with a girl and he wanted to impress her, so all through the evening he talked about himself. He told her about his career, bragged about the favourable reviews he had received for his last performance and he talked in glowing terms about his future prospects. The girl was getting very bored and fed up with all this. Noticing this at last, the boy turned to her and said, 'Well, that's enough about me. Now let's talk about you. What did you think of me in my last role?'

STORY 2

The second story is about a woman who was continually gossiping about others. She told her friends something unpleasant about a new family that had moved into the street. It turned out to be completely false, but the harm was done. By this time just about everyone in the village had heard this detrimental story, all because of one woman and her habit of gossiping. Aware that she had caused a lot of distress by what she had done, she confessed all to the priest and asked his advice. He said that she should go and apologise to the family concerned and then get a chicken from the farm. It should be a fresh chicken that still had all its feathers. She was to pluck the chicken and put the feathers in a bag. Her task was then to go around the village placing a feather on the doorstep of each house. She duly completed the task and reported this fact to the priest. He was pleased she had taken his advice and said that she should now go around again and collect them up. The woman set off, bag in hand, but she soon realised the hopelessness of the task. By this time the feathers had blown away and it was quite impossible to get them back. She returned to tell the priest that the task he had set her this time was quite impossible. 'Precisely,' the priest replied, 'and that is what happens when you gossip about people. Once you have spread the stories around, there is no way you can take them back.' The damage has been done. The woman learned her lesson and never gossiped about people again.

REFLECTION/RESPONSE

There is a well-known saying that when you point the finger at someone else there are three pointing back at you. Have there been times when you have criticised someone else for something that you have been guilty of yourself? If so, you might like to think about the consequences such action might bring and reflect on the importance of recognising one's own faults.

TO THINK ABOUT

Do you have a family member or a friend you trust who would be willing to help you recognise any weaknesses or faults and support you as you try to deal with them?

36

THEME

Animal Magic

FOCUS

The relationship between God, people and animals.

SUMMARY

In this assembly we look at two stories about animals. One is about an elephant that helped to build a hospital and the other is about a donkey that talked.

RESOURCES

OHTs of the elephant and the donkey.

PREPARATION REQUIRED

None.

TALK

How many of you have an animal of some kind that you or your family keeps as a pet? Most people love animals and look after their pets. Sometimes they are treated like an important member of the family. Has anyone here got a donkey or an elephant for a pet? I expect we have all seen a donkey in real life, and most of us have probably seen an elephant

either at a zoo or on TV. In this morning's assembly we are going to hear two short stories, one about an elephant and one about a donkey.

The first story is about an elephant that helped to build a hospital *(put up OHT of elephant)*. This is a young African elephant who lived in the bush near a place called Tumutumu. One day he was out in the hills in that district when he spotted a white man who was carrying a gun. He looked like a hunter. The young elephant knew instinctively that this spelt trouble. He realised that his life and the life of his family and friends could be in danger if this man was able to get close enough to them. Without stopping to think, the young elephant rushed at the hunter. The hunter heard the elephant approaching and went for his gun. He lifted it to fire at the charging elephant, but the safety catch jammed and he couldn't get the gun to fire. All the hunter could do was to seize the tusks of the young elephant as it came at him.

The elephant came down on him, driving its tusks into the ground beside the man. The elephant must have thought he had killed the hunter and he lumbered off to rejoin his companions. The group of people with the hunter had also run off. They thought he was dead too. The hunter wasn't dead, but he was badly injured and was knocked unconscious by the blow he had received. Some time later, the hunter came round and started to shout for help. One of the bearers who had been with the hunter came back and saw that the hunter was still alive, although badly injured. He went off to get help. He returned with a doctor who was able to help the man and get him back to the village where he looked after him and helped him to make a full recovery.

The hunter was an American who had plenty of money and some rich sponsors behind him. They had a plan to build a great museum that would house a collection of big animals. The hunter's job was to find, kill and ship home as many big animals as he could. The doctor who saved the hunter's life came from Scotland and he had been sent out to Africa by the Church of Scotland to help provide some medical care for the people in the Tumutumu district. So, one man had come to take life and one had come to save life. Fortunately, when the hunter had regained his strength and was able to return home, he asked the doctor if there was some way he could help him with his work. He wanted to do something to repay the doctor for saving his life. They talked long into the night, and eventually the hunter decided that he would donate a large sum of money to allow the doctor to build a small hospital in Tumutumu. The hospital played an important part in bringing health and healing to the people of that area. Many people also heard about the gospel of Jesus from the doctor. So, in a way, it was thanks to the elephant who charged down the hunter that the hospital at Tumutumu was built.

There are many stories about animals that show how they can, sometimes without knowing it, play an important part in helping people or even saving a person's life. There is even a story in the Bible about a donkey who talked. The story is in the book of Numbers in the Old Testament. It involves a man called Balaam who was also setting out on a journey. God had told him not to go on this journey, but Balaam didn't listen and he set off on his donkey (OHT). Things seemed to be going well, until the donkey suddenly veered off the road into a field.

Balaam thought it was just a case of his donkey being very stubborn, as they can be at times. He started to beat the donkey in an attempt to get it to go back onto the pathway. The donkey did start to go forward again, but then it swerved into the side

179

of the narrow road, crushing Balaam's foot against the wall. Balaam was very angry by now and could see no reason why the donkey was playing up like this. A third time the donkey stopped, and this time he lay down in the road. Balaam beat the animal again. However, according to the story, the donkey had seen something up ahead that his master hadn't seen. An angel of the Lord with a sword in his hand was blocking the road. Balaam continued to beat the donkey, unaware of the angel's presence.

Finally, we read that the donkey actually spoke to Balaam and asked him what he had done to him to make him beat him like this. Balaam must have been shocked! Eventually, Balaam stopped mistreating his animal and saw the angel for himself. Then God spoke to Balaam and told him what he must do. The donkey, it seems, had more sense than his master and was used by God to help Balaam see where he was going wrong.[1]

REFLECTION/RESPONSE

Let us think quietly about the joy and pleasure animals can bring into our lives. Some of you may like to thank God silently in a simple prayer for the variety of animals in our world and the benefits they bring to us. You may even like to thank God that he sometimes uses animals and our pets to bring us closer to him or to teach us a lesson that we would find hard to accept any other way.

TO THINK ABOUT

Do you think God can work through animals to help people or show them important things?

NOTES

1. Edgar Primrose Dickie, 'The elephant who built a hospital', adapted from *A Second Year's Talks to Children* (Hodder and Stoughton: London, 1943).

37

How Does Your Garden Grow?

FOCUS

The wonder and beauty of a well-kept garden.

SUMMARY

This assembly tells the story of one small boy's efforts to produce a prize-winning garden and refers to the Garden of Gethsemane frequented by Jesus. It uses the analogy of a garden to provoke a positive response of wonder at the colour, beauty and variety of nature.

RESOURCES

Some flowerpots, gardening gloves, trowel, seeds, etc.

PREPARATION REQUIRED

None.

TALK

Does anyone here like gardening? I've got my gardening gloves, some seeds and some pots if anyone is interested in giving me a hand. Perhaps some of you have a garden of your own or you may go round and help a neighbour with their garden. Some people are mad about gardening, aren't they? They watch all the TV programmes about gardening, they listen to *Gardeners' Question Time* every week, they buy magazines about gardening and the local garden centre is like their second home! Perhaps someone here is an aspiring Alan Titchmarsh or Pippa Greenwood? Some people just seem to have 'green fingers' and can get anything to grow, while others can't even manage to grow a cabbage successfully! But most people will agree that a beautiful garden can be an inspiration and a place of escape. It has been said that 'one is nearer to God in a garden than anywhere else on earth'.

From the earliest times, gardens have featured in history. When Arab armies conquered parts of Spain in the eighth century, they brought with them a love of gardening and a passion for plants. The Koran teaches that it is humankind's duty to conserve plant life — which has a divine creator. Gardens were looked on as a reflection of the beauty and tranquillity of heaven. They called them *Paradeisoi* — paradises. Instructions to advancing soldiers included orders not to cut down any palm trees or destroy any orchard or burn any cornfield. The Arabs, like many others, revered the natural world as the work of the Almighty. Most people's ideas about paradise include an idealistic picture of rolling hills, flower-filled meadows, trees swaying in the breeze and a gentle flowing stream. Birds sing, insects are busy about their work and the air is full of perfume from the beautiful array of flowers and shrubs. For many people, a garden is a place of peace and tranquillity. A place to escape from the hustle and bustle of modern life.

In a school in West Africa, the boys were taught

gardening skills from a young age and every year there was a competition for the best garden. One seven-year-old boy was keen to enter the junior competition. He worked hard preparing his patch of ground and putting in the seeds. He dug them up a couple of times to see how they were doing, but eventually the shoots came through and the seedlings began to grow — until one of the turkeys escaped from its pen and scratched up all his plants. He was not to be beaten though, so he started all over again. This time the seeds came up and he had some fine rows of flowers and vegetables that should be at their best by the time the gardens were judged for the competition. The boy was excited. He felt he had a good chance of winning.

Then the boy fell ill, so ill that he had to go into the school's medical centre for treatment and nursing care. From his bed, the boy could see other boys passing to and from the gardens. The weather was hot and dry and he was sure that by now his flowers would have wilted and his plot would be full of weeds. The turkey had probably escaped again and ruined anything that was left. He imagined the other boys laughing at his overgrown garden and brushed away a tear from his cheek. He would never win the prize now.

Finally, the doctor said that he was well enough to go outside for the first time for several weeks. He wandered along to the gardens expecting the worse. As he got near his plot, he could see that all the flowers looked beautiful, the vegetables were fine and there was hardly a weed in sight! He realised now that the boys he had seen passing by his hospital window were in fact going to look after his plot, as well as their own. Then, at the top of his garden he saw there was a stick on which there was a red card. He went for a closer look. He could hardly believe his eyes. It read: 'Garden Competition: First

183

Prize'. The other boys had decided that he deserved to win and they weren't going to let a little thing like his illness stop him getting what was rightfully his.

There are several references to gardens in the Bible. The first, of course, is the garden of Eden. This was a beautiful garden planted by God for the enjoyment of his creation. No weeds grew there and the earth was watered by nightly dew. Another famous garden in the Bible is the garden of Gethsemane. This was a garden just outside Jerusalem, which was often visited by Jesus. The word 'Gethsemane' probably comes from an Aramaic word meaning 'oil press' because there were olive trees growing there from which the olives would be taken and crushed to make olive oil. The garden was on the slopes of the Mount of Olives, just across the Kidron valley, not far from the road that led into the city through the Golden Gate.

The Gospel writers tell us that Jesus went to this garden after eating his final meal with his disciples. It was here that he prayed before being arrested and led off to stand trial and eventual crucifixion. Still today, pilgrims visit the area still known by the name of Gethsemane where there is a lovely garden tended by the Franciscans. Ancient, gnarled olive trees can be seen there, along with a selection of plants and sweet-smelling flowers. Not far away, one can see the walls of the old city of Jerusalem. No doubt Jesus went to this garden to get away from the crowds and the noise of the city and to pray quietly or sit and think about things, in much the same way as people use gardens or parks today.

REFLECTION/RESPONSE

Plato's prayer for true wisdom (see below) could be put up on an OHT so that pupils have the opportunity to reflect on the content and thoughts expressed there.

Beloved God of woods and streams, grant us to be beautiful in the inner man, and all we have of outer things to be at peace with those within. Counting only the wise to be truly rich, increase to all who here abide their store of that true gold.
(Plato, 427–347 BC, from the *Phaedrus*)

TO THINK ABOUT

How much do you notice and appreciate the wonder and beauty of the world around you?

38

Go Forward

FOCUS

Leaving the past behind.

SUMMARY

This assembly is about the dangers of living in the past by making happy memories a substitute for progress.

RESOURCES

A plank of wood and a blindfold.

PREPARATION REQUIRED

None.

TALK

(Begin by asking for two or three volunteers to come to the front to walk across a plank of wood which is laid across the floor. Build up interest with comments like, 'You will have to do this without any assistance.' Let each pupil 'walk the plank' in turn then ask him or her to do the same thing again, but this time wearing a blindfold. Applaud each pupil as they complete the task.)

Walking across a plank of wood placed on the floor is neither dangerous nor difficult. Some of you can even do it blindfolded! But, if I were to place this same plank of wood twenty feet above the ground, you would probably not be so keen to have a go at walking across it. Why is that? You would use the same muscles, the same mind and the same skills. The difference is that when the plank is on the ground, you would be thinking only about walking across the plank, but if the plank was suspended twenty feet up in the air, you would be thinking more about falling!

This is an illustration of the way some people think about life. They see all the problems and let the things that worry or frighten them stop them from moving on towards their goal. They are thinking more about falling off than staying on. It is impossible to make real progress when you are looking at the ditch into which you may fall.

Another reason why some people do not move on in life is because they spend all their time looking back at past successes. They are so caught up with their memories of the past that they take no action now. An old fable about a flock of geese illustrates this point.

A flock of geese lived in a farmyard. They enjoyed their life there and often passed the time by getting together in a corner of the farmyard to listen to one of their flock as he talked about their ancestors and told stories of their wonderful past. He would inspire them with stories about their exploits as they flew thousands of miles each winter to find warmer weather and a place to spend the winter months. He would talk about the ability of these geese to fly for thousands of miles in order to find a suitable home. He spoke of their stamina and their will to go on, even when there were dangers and their strength had almost gone. As they listened to these stories, the geese would nod their heads and talk proudly about their ancestors' fine accomplishments. They did everything proud geese should do, except one thing — they never flew themselves. You see, they had forgotten how to fly! Each time the meeting ended, they would go back to the security of their farmyard where they knew there would be good corn to eat and shelter from the winter winds. They had become so dependent on the farmer looking after their needs that they lost the will and the ability to follow their instinct to soar above the farmyard to seek food, a place to shelter and new and exciting experiences. It was much easier and safer to stay in the farmyard. They were content to substitute happy memories for action.

Some people are like these geese. They would rather sit around and let others do the work and make the plans than get involved themselves. They prefer to talk about past successes than work towards fresh achievements and new goals. They see only the risks and are frightened of failure.

David Scott Blackhall was blind, but he did not let this stop him attempting to climb Scotland's highest mountain, Ben Nevis, along with a group of fifteen other blind 'would-be' climbers. They met up in Fort William to finalise their plans for the planned ascent the next day. They were to be accompanied by nearly as many sighted guides and three guide dogs. At nine-thirty on the next day, they arrived at the foot of the mountain ready to start the climb. They proceeded single file with the guides and experts placed at strategic points along the line. Some of the blind climbers were latched loosely to a guide, but walked unaided once they were sure that they were moving in the right direction along the path. The sighted guides faced a challenge too, but they began to grow in confidence when one of them slipped and was caught by one of the blind members of the group who was sensitive to his plight. They walked on. Eventually, they reached a ford in the rushing mountain river. The guides had to heave more boulders into the water to enable the group to attempt a crossing. The noise of the river drowned out the voices of the instructors, but everyone made it safely across.

They pressed on into the rain clouds with increased determination. Alone, they might have turned back, but no one was willing to let the rest of the group down. At the halfway point, they stopped to rest and enjoyed the flasks of piping hot coffee they had brought with them. One of their number who was also diabetic, confessed at this point that he had twisted his knee and that he had better go back. One of the guides was assigned to see him safely back to base. The others moved on. The track was becoming rougher now with loose scree under their feet. Their physical resources were being stretched, but they had the will power to go on. Another of the party had to admit defeat at three and a half thousand feet. The rest pressed on, determined to make it to the top. At four thousand feet, they emerged from the rain cloud with another four hundred feet to go. It was more a case of pride that would keep them united in their resolve to make it to the top. Finally, tired, wet and cold, they stood on the topmost rock as one of the party struck up a drone on the wettest of bagpipes to announce their arrival at the summit. Fourteen of the original group of blind climbers had made it.[1]

REFLECTION/RESPONSE

It is often easier to stay where you are in life rather than take the risk of going forward and attempting something new. It takes a lot of grit and determination to do something like that group of blind climbers, but together they reached their goal.

There are those here today who are facing a fresh challenge of some sort. It may be a new piece of work, or a fresh opportunity waiting to be taken up. Perhaps you feel unequal to the task. You have experienced success in the past, but this challenge seems a step too far. If you are feeling like that, then remember that there are others, like the guides in the story, who are willing to go with you and help you reach your goal.

In the book of Deuteronomy in the Old Testament, God told the children of Israel on their journey from Egypt to the promised land that they had made their way around the mountain long enough. Now it was time to go north and move on. It was time for them to go forward, with his help.[2]

TO THINK ABOUT

It is said that 'two men looked through prison bars; one saw mud the other stars'. What do you see from where you are right now?

NOTES
1. David Scott Blackhall, 'The Way I see it', in Michael Davis, *More Words for Worship* (Edward Arnold, 1980).
2. Deuteronomy 2:3.

39

<u>THEME</u>

It Could Be You!

FOCUS

> The excitement and dangers of playing the Lottery.

SUMMARY

> This assembly seeks to highlight some of the dangers of playing the Lottery and gambling in general. It invites pupils to consider the importance of making the most of life rather than living with a 'pipe dream'.

RESOURCES

> None.

PREPARATION REQUIRED

> None.

TALK

> I'm sure you have all seen the advert on TV for the National Lottery where a big hand comes down from the sky pointing straight at you as a booming voice declares, 'It could be you!' Of course, if you are old enough to be able to play the Lottery and if you have selected your numbers and bought your ticket,

then it could be you. The chances of you scooping one of the really big prizes are very small, however, and the people most likely to benefit from the money paid for the ticket are the Lottery organisers and then a few chosen charities.

The advent of a National Lottery did not please a lot of people, who think that encouraging people to gamble in this way or raising money for good causes through a lottery is not a good way of raising funds. Many Church leaders have spoken out against the Lottery, but there seems to be little chance of us losing it when it is clear that so many people play the Lottery every week. The excitement of listening each time to the winning numbers being drawn is enough to make some people buy their ticket every week. The idea that they might suddenly find themselves with more money than they know what to do with is a powerful one. Twice a week the nation holds its breath as the machine spits out the winning numbers. This week, someone will be lucky. Someone will be tempted to throw in their job and live a life of ease and luxury. But is winning the Lottery all it's cracked up to be, or is there a down side to this issue?

It seems from the evidence presented by some researchers, that for many people doing the Lottery is not a source of pleasure but a trap from which they feel unable to escape. Why is this? Well, it seems that out of the 30 million people who regularly play the Lottery every week, about 56% play the same set of numbers every week. This means that if they do not buy a ticket for either of the weekly draws, they stand the risk of their usual numbers coming up just on the very day they didn't buy a ticket! Some of the 485 people questioned about this in a survey admitted that they were scared silly of missing a draw — 'just in case!' For people playing the same numbers each week, just to hear the draw is a relief from worrying about a missed draw. For the same kind of reasons, many people fear the introduction of a third or even fourth draw each week as it will mean buying yet more tickets to make sure their combination is not drawn on a day when they didn't buy a ticket.

When the National Lottery first started in Britain, most people spent £1 or £2 a week on it, but now with the introduction of a mid-week draw, average spending has increased to £6 a week. So where's the harm in it? Of course, many people can afford to put out that kind of money each week and they can console themselves with the thought that some of it will be going to good causes. However, for some families this is money they really need for other purposes. Research shows that 64% of people playing the Saturday draw do so because they feel a compulsion to do so, while only 21% played the Lottery because they enjoyed it.

Another reason why some people are against the Lottery and other forms of gambling and 'get-rich-quick' schemes is because they feel that they go against values like hard work, encouraging attitudes of greed and selfishness.

But what of those who do win? Are they happy? It seems that some of them do not find instant or long-term happiness through winning the Lottery. Some people say that they did not win enough to get what they would really like in life — like an island of their own in the sun or an airline which would be all theirs and carry their name. Others are actually frightened about claiming a big win. One eighty-nine-year-old lady wrote to her local paper (using only her first name) to say that she had a winning Lottery ticket sitting on the table in her front room. If this was true, the prize she could have claimed was £2,540,754. She went on to say that her husband had bought the ticket unbeknown to her and had never gambled in his life, as far as she knew. She didn't know what had made him buy the ticket, but before he could claim his win he had died in hospital after a long illness. Now, his widow did not feel it right to claim the prize. She said it would have been different if she could have her life over again, but that it was too late for it to be of any use to her now. If left unclaimed, the prize money would join the other unclaimed prizes and eventually be given away to charity. She was frightened of suddenly having so much money and the notoriety it would bring with it. Perhaps she was wise. What do you think?

REFLECTION/RESPONSE

It has been said that money doesn't buy happiness. Most people would probably agree with this statement, but would still like the chance to find out!

There is a story of a man who others called poor, but he had just enough to support himself and journey around the country on occasions. The story goes that one day he was in the company of a great millionaire who had a business which was growing and making him richer by the day. The poor man fell into conversation with the millionaire and soon found that he was not a happy person. 'Why,' said the poor man, 'I am richer than you are.' 'How do you make that out?' the rich man replied. 'Well, I have got as much money as I want, and you haven't,' replied the poor man.

TO THINK ABOUT

A recent report on the Lottery suggests that it is not a source of pleasure, but an inescapable trap for some people. What does this mean?

40

<u>THEME</u>

Here Is the News

FOCUS

Responding to good and bad news.

SUMMARY

This assembly uses three short and simple sketches to look at a variety of ways news can be relayed, different sorts of news that may be brought to us and how we respond to that news.

RESOURCES

Table and two chairs for sketch one. Sealed envelopes containing an exam result for sketch two. A telephone for the third sketch.

PREPARATION REQUIRED

Practise the sketches.

TALK

Have you heard people say, 'What do you want first, the good news or the bad news?' Which would you choose? None of us like receiving bad news, so perhaps you would choose to get that out of the way first so that you have the good news to look forward to afterwards. Whichever you choose, there is no getting away from the fact that there are different sorts of news, some good, some bad, and we have to cope with it whatever it is.

The way a piece of news is conveyed often depends on the type of message and what it is about. Some pupils are going to show us how different items of news may be relayed:

SKETCH 1: A TV NEWS PROGRAMME
(Two news-readers seated at a desk take turns to read out the main world news item.)

Reader 1: Good morning and welcome to the programme. First, news is coming in about a major earthquake in Afghanistan. Measuring a massive 7.1 on the Richter scale, it struck the same area of remote northern Afghanistan that was devastated by another earthquake in February, which killed 3,000 people and left thousands more homeless. News about this latest disaster is beginning to filter out, but no one can be sure of the true scale of the disaster yet, as it is difficult to reach the stricken area, which is one of the remotest places in the world. Conservative estimates put the death toll from this latest tragedy at 4,000 people killed and many more injured, although this number looks set to rise when the true scale of the tragedy becomes known.

Reader 2: The quake was centred on the Takhar and Shari Basarkh region where at least fifty villages have been destroyed. Simple mud homes, many of them weakened by the February quake, simply collapsed without warning as the quake struck. Access to the area is difficult, but helicopters have been flying over the area and relief operations are already under way. With 45,000 being made homeless by the latest quake, the most urgent need is for tents, plastic sheeting and medical supplies. The priority is to treat the injured, most of which are women and children. We will bring you up to date with the latest news from the area with a report from our correspondent who is in the area later in the programme.

Reader 1: And now the rest of the news headlines. Football star Paul Gascoigne is being pursued by the press this morning after Hoddle's shock decision to leave him out of the England World Cup Squad.

SKETCH 2

(This requires two people to play the role of a mother and son and shows someone receiving an examination result.)

Mum: This has just arrived for you Sam *(hands over unopened envelope with a piece of paper inside).* I think it might be your exam result. I hope it's good news!

Dan: Thanks Mum. Oh, I don't really want to open it. I'm sure I didn't pass. You won't be mad with me will you. I did my best, really!

Mum: Come on, you haven't opened it yet. Perhaps you have passed. You worked hard for it and I think you deserved to pass anyway.

Dan: I know, but I was really nervous and I had to start one piece three times before I got it right. You don't know what it was like in there.

Mum: All right, all right. Calm down! Why don't you just open it and see.

Dan: Will you do it? I don't think I can.

Mum: (Takes envelope and starts opening it to read the result inside.) OK. I guess someone's got to do it.

Dan: Well, come on... give me the bad news.

Mum: Bad news? What bad news? You passed... with merit! *(Hugs all round!)*

SKETCH 3: TELEPHONE CONVERSATION
(The telephone rings. Tim answers it and has the following conversation with a friend.)

Tim: Phil! Hi! What's going on? *(Pauses for reply.)* Cancelled? What d'you mean, cancelled? *(Wait for reply.)* But that's not on. Surely they can't cancel the trip now. We've already booked the tickets. *(Pause.)* I know, but that's not the same as going on Saturday. That won't be half as good a match and I've been saving up for this for ages. I'd rather not go at all. What about the tickets? Do you think we can get our money back? *(Pause.)* OK then. I'll ring you back when I've found out. 'Bye. *(Hangs up.)*

TALK

Our three sketches have shown us three different ways we can receive good and bad news. News about events around the world or in our own area can be relayed to us over the TV or radio or through our newspapers. We can also receive news about a variety of topics through a FAX, e-mail or even via the Internet. News of a more personal sort is more likely to reach us by word of mouth, through the post or by way of a telephone call.

REFLECTION/RESPONSE

Modern forms of communication mean that receiving news is a daily event for most of us. Many of the messages we receive require a response. For example, we might respond to news that someone we care about is very ill by sending a get-well card. News of a good exam result might mean organising a party to celebrate.

We may not be so quick to respond to other sorts of news about people we don't know or that relate to something which is happening hundreds of miles away. Pictures or graphic descriptions of the latest disaster in Africa or Afghanistan regularly feature in the news and some people seem able just to 'switch-off' to such tragedies because they have 'seen it all before' or because it doesn't have any direct effect on them. Most of us are moved by real need when we see it. Appeals for money to help people facing a crisis by organisations like 'Comic Relief' or 'Children in Need' regularly raise millions of pounds for such causes. Aid agencies often work around the clock to help in the provision of emergency relief to people around the world as news of the latest crisis reaches us in the West, but they are limited in what they can do by the lack of funds and the need for more support from people like us.

Their message to us today would probably be, 'Don't turn away.' There is something we can do, however small it may seem.

TO THINK ABOUT

How do you respond when you receive good news and how do you respond to bad news?

41

<u>THEME</u>

Breakfast and the Blue Sky

FOCUS

Greed.

SUMMARY

The main element of this assembly is a story about a greedy goat who became so discontented with his own food that he decided to go in search of a more varied and fulfilling diet — with tragic consequences. The assembly challenges pupils to think about real situations where people are more concerned about building up their own resources than sharing what they have with others who have much less.

RESOURCES

OHT of the drawing of the goat and other animals.

PREPARATION REQUIRED

None.

TALK

One sunny morning in a field of long grass, near a wood, under a sycamore tree, a goat slept a long and

deep sleep. When he awoke, he watched clouds floating past in the blue sky for a while and then he thought, 'Hmm, I'm really very hungry,' so he went to a cabbage patch he knew and ate and ate until there were only a few tough stalks left. 'Well, I'm still hungry,' thought Goat, 'I'll go and see Horse. He's always got food.' And off he went to visit Horse.

'Good morning Horse,' said Goat. 'Good morning Goat,' said Horse. 'Do you have any food, Horse?' Goat asked. Horse replied, 'Yes. I have some carrots I was just about to eat. Would you like to share them?' Goat thanked Horse for his hospitality and they ate up all the carrots. 'I'm still hungry, Horse,' said Goat. 'So am I,' said Horse. 'Shall we go and visit Cow?' suggested Goat. 'She's always got some food.' Horse agreed and so they went to visit Cow.

'Good morning Cow,' said Goat and Horse. 'Good morning Goat. Good morning Horse,' said Cow. 'We're hungry, Cow. Do you have any food?' Goat asked Cow. 'Well,' said Cow, 'I do have some apples I was about to have for my breakfast. Would you like to join me? We could share them out.' Goat and Horse thanked Cow for her hospitality and they shared out the apples. After they had finished eating Goat said, 'I'm still hungry.' 'Yes, those apples didn't go very far,' said Cow. 'We could go and visit Sheep,' suggested Goat. 'She has always got something to eat.' So Horse and Cow agreed to go and visit Sheep.

'Good morning Sheep,' said Goat, Horse and Cow. 'Good morning Goat. Good morning Horse. Good morning Cow,' said Sheep. 'Do you have any food, Sheep?' asked Goat. 'Yes, I do. I've some turnips. Would you like to share them with me?' Sheep asked. Goat, Horse and Cow all thanked Sheep for her hospitality and they all shared the turnips. When they had finished, Goat said, 'I'm certainly not hungry any more. I'm so full, I think I must lie down for a while.' 'Well, I'm still hungry,' exclaimed Horse. 'So am I,' said Cow. 'Me too,' said Sheep.

Just then, Tiger came along. 'Good morning all,' said Tiger waving one of his huge paws. 'Good morning Tiger,' said Goat, Horse, Cow and Sheep. 'We're all hungry, Tiger,' Sheep told him. 'Hmm, so am I,' growled Tiger checking his claws were clean and sharp ready for his breakfast. As Tiger was saying this, Sheep, Cow, Horse and Goat became very nervous. After a few long seconds while Tiger eyed them all, his mouth started to water, Sheep spoke up. 'Well, I'd love to stand around chatting all day, but I really do have a very important...err...' and ran away as fast as her feet would carry her. Cow then announced, 'Umm, I also have a very important...err...' and sped off after Sheep. 'Me too,' said Horse, and galloped off to catch up with Sheep and Cow.

Although Tiger was still there, Goat suddenly felt very alone. 'Are you staying for breakfast?' Tiger asked him. Goat was too full to run away. 'I am already full, thank you,' replied Goat. 'Good,' said Tiger, 'You won't mind if I carry on then?' Goat did mind, but he had no choice. He made a very filling breakfast for Tiger. When he was full, Tiger spent the rest of his day lying in the long grass, mostly sleeping, but occasionally watching clouds floating past in the blue sky.[1]

REFLECTION/RESPONSE

Perhaps Goat got what he deserved. After all, he was the one who started it all. Goat's greedy ways brought him to a sad end.

There are some people around who are like Goat in that they are not content with what they have. They roam around looking for more and seize on any opportunity they find to satisfy their craving for more.

Some would say that the countries of the West are a bit like Goat, too. They have more than enough food and money to satisfy their needs, but they are not content with that. They continually harass other poor countries (that have had to borrow from the rich countries just to survive), to repay huge debts which they cannot afford to pay back.

Jubilee 2000 has been set up to give a voice to the thousands of people in this country who want to protest about this situation. More than 70,000 people from across the country gathered in Birmingham to let their feelings be known to world leaders who were gathering there for the G8 conference. As they discussed the growing problem of Third World debt, the campaigners linked hands forming a human chain around the city to symbolise the chains of debt that hang around the necks of some of the poorest nations on the face of the planet. Jubilee 2000 campaigners want countries to mark the millennium by cancelling all Third World debts so that conditions in those countries can be improved. The campaign has already made an impact with the British Government now working with Uganda to reduce its debts. One campaigner at the Birmingham rally expressed the feelings of many when she said that she had to join the protest because she had heard that the United Nations predicts that 21 million children will die as a direct result of the problems caused by Third World debt. Others said they had joined Jubilee 2000 because they felt it was wrong that tens of millions of people continue to live in absolute poverty because of their country's debts.[2] What do you think? Is this a good idea?

TO THINK ABOUT

Do you agree with the idea that the rich nations of the West should cancel these debts?

NOTES

1. Britton Matthew, 'Breakfast and the Blue Sky', unpublished work.
2. From an article, 'Protesters for Jubilee 2000 vow to fight on', (Guardian and Gazette, June 4th 1998), p. 23.

42

<u>THEME</u>

True Greatness

FOCUS

Characteristics of a truly great person.

SUMMARY

This assembly looks at different people's ideas about what makes a person 'great' in the sense of being wise, of good character and respected by those who know them best.

RESOURCES

A line and some clothes pegs. Large sheets of card or stiff paper each bearing one of the following words: COURAGE, PERSEVERANCE, WHOLEHEARTED-NESS, INTEGRITY, ENTHUSIASM, TEAMWORK, KINDNESS, HUMILITY.

PREPARATION REQUIRED

Write the captions. Practise the readers if necessary.

TALK

(The line should be tied across the front of the assembly at a safe height, but still within reach so that each of

the captions can be pegged to it as you go through the assembly.)

Here is a question for you: What do you think are the marks of true greatness? *(Take a few answers if they are offered, otherwise continue.)* Let's see what qualities different people, some of whom were great people themselves, identified as being marks of a truly great person.

(As you go through each characteristic, peg your caption on the line as a pupil reads out the paragraph on each one.)

1. COURAGE

'Today we need a special kind of courage, not the kind needed in battle, but a kind which makes us stand up for everything that we know is right, everything that is true and honest.' *(Queen Elizabeth II in her first Christmas television broadcast)*

2. PERSEVERANCE

'Enter upon your inheritance, accept your responsibilities. Don't take "No" for an answer. Never submit to failure. You will make mistakes; but as long as you are generous and true, and also fierce, you cannot hurt the world or even seriously distress her. She was made to be wooed and won by youth.' *(Winston Churchill)*

3. WHOLEHEARTEDNESS

'Rugby football is fast and exciting. It is a chance to be daring. When I first played at school, I tackled half-heartedly and got hurt. I blamed the game. Then one day I did it with determination, and found it was easy. I began to enjoy the game. This is an important lesson for life. Whole-heartedness is the way.' *(Brian Boobbyer)*

4. INTEGRITY

'There are three qualities you must have if you are going to succeed finally, however technically proficient you may be. First you must have integrity, which I would say in your own profession (of commerce) is particularly important. Second you must have courage, not necessarily physical courage, but moral courage, standing firm by what one believes to be right.'

5. ENTHUSIASM

'Third, you must have enthusiasm, the ability to get something out of life by putting something into it in an enthusiastic way.' *(Field Marshall the Viscount Montgomery of Alamein in a talk given to students at the London School of Commerce)*

6. TEAMWORK

'In this or any other mountain venture, sound and successful climbing is fundamentally a matter of teamwork. A particular route on our home crags or on a mountain of alpine dimension may safely be climbed by no more than two men, unsupported by any others. Yet even they comprise a team; they are linked by a rope which does more than provide mutual security — it symbolises their unity of purpose.' *(Sir John Hunt on the climbing of Everest)*

7. KINDNESS

'Doing nothing for others is the undoing of one's self. We must be purposely kind and generous, or we miss the best part of existence. The heart that goes out of itself, gets large and full of joy. This is the great secret of the inner life. We do ourselves the most good doing something for others.' *(Horace Mann)*

8. HUMILITY

'Some of the greatest men I have had the privilege of knowing not only are the most humble, but are those who express their humility by becoming actual servants in their relationships with others.' *(Mark O. Hatfield)*

Of course there are many more things one could suggest are necessary for true greatness, but time will not permit us to go through them all. The words of such great people as Winston Churchill and Her Majesty the Queen are good for us to ponder, but the following definition from a little American girl might be worth thinking about too.

'Once there was a woman who had done a big wash and hung it on the line. The line broke and the washing fell in the mud, but the woman didn't say a word, only did it all over again. This time she spread it on the grass, where it couldn't fall. But that night a dog ran over it with his muddy feet.

'When she saw what had happened she sat down and didn't cry a bit. All she said was, "Ain't it queer that he didn't miss nothing?" That was true greatness, but it is only people who have done washing that know it.'

REFLECTION/RESPONSE

The lesson in this little story must be that whoever we are and however insignificant our task, the important thing is the attitude in which we come to it. We need to keep our minds focused on the job in hand and keep at it, even when discouragement and setbacks come. It is important not to give up and to take a positive view.

John Ruskin said that really great people have a curious feeling that the greatness is not in them but through them, and that they see something divine in every other man and woman and are endlessly, foolishly and incredibly merciful.

As we reflect on the ideas we have heard about what makes true greatness *(point to line of captions)*, some of you may like to show your agreement with the following prayer by adding your 'Amen' to it in the appropriate place.

O Father, who has taught us through Jesus Christ that the greatest people are those who forget themselves in the service of others; grant us grace to learn this hard lesson of self-forgetfulness, so that we may live to make others great. Amen.

TO THINK ABOUT

No person can achieve true greatness, who can count their enemies on their fingers.

43

Fear

FOCUS

Facing our fears.

SUMMARY

This assembly takes a silly story about a tiger as the basis for looking at things that frighten us and ways of facing or overcoming our fears.

RESOURCES

None.

PREPARATION REQUIRED

None.

TALK

Many years ago there lived a man in India who earned his living as a conjurer and juggler. He would go about the country performing his tricks and making just enough money to get by on.

One evening, he was walking through a clearing in the forest, when he saw a tiger lurking in the bushes, sharpening its claws. It looked hungry. As soon as the tiger saw the man coming towards him, his thoughts turned to supper and he was after the man in an instant. Knowing how fast a tiger can run, the man decided his only hope of escape lay in climbing the first tree he could reach. He set off at great speed, but soon realised that he would never make the tree in time. The tiger was gaining on him with every step. Then he had a brilliant idea. Up ahead he saw a small ridge and he knew that if he could get over it, he would be out of the tiger's sight for a few seconds. This was his only chance. As soon as he was over the ridge he stopped and began to do one of the tricks he did to amuse people. He spread out his legs as far as he could, then he curled his head down between his knees so that he was looking backwards through his legs. Then he stretched out his arms above him like the sails of a windmill and began to wave them round and round with all his might.

As the tiger came bounding over the ridge, the man let out a blood-curdling yell, such as no tiger had ever heard before. The tiger stopped in its tracks. What was this? He had never seen or heard anything like it in his life. In front of him was a fierce windmill shaped monster with its head in the middle of its body and its mouth actually above its glaring eyes. Its limbs were swinging round and round waiting to catch its prey. It must have already eaten the man the tiger was chasing because there was no sign of him. The tiger didn't hang around to think things over. He turned tail and headed back towards the jungle!

Now you and I might laugh at the tiger. We might call him stupid and think that we would never have been taken in by such a silly trick. But I'm not so sure about that. Things we don't understand, or have never come across before easily scare most of us. How often have you put off doing something or going somewhere because you haven't been there or done that particular thing before?

Like the tiger, some people also have fears about things that there is no real reason to be frightened about. We might call these superstitions. Some people think Friday 13 is an unlucky day. Others tell you something dreadful will happen to you if you spill the salt and that it's unlucky to walk under a ladder or see a black bird outside your window. Sometimes our fears do have some kind of foundation. If you have had a bad experience of something in the past, you are more scared of facing that thing again in the future. Some people feel like this about a visit to the dentist. One dentist had a well-known lawyer come to his surgery for treatment. As the lawyer got into the dentist's chair, the dentist realised that the man was trembling. He decided to leave the man for a moment so that he could compose himself. He went into the next room on the pretext of getting something. When the dentist came back, the chair was empty and the lawyer had fled the surgery!

Perhaps some people here get frightened about certain things we have to face even here in school. It is easy to feel apprehensive about starting a new school, joining a new class or taking a test or exam. Sometimes pupils get so worked up about something like this that they decide to do what that lawyer did and make a run for it! But running away from a problem rarely does anything to solve it, as some of us know. Better to face the problem and ask someone to help us get through it than to turn tail, like that tiger did, and run away.

REFLECTION/RESPONSE

I am told that in the centre of the great city of Edinburgh, you can see the grave of a man called John Knox. This man experienced many hardships and problems in his life. He was sent as a slave to a French galley where, chained to oars, he had no escape from the boat, the elements or the whip of the slave driver. Yet no one could break this man's spirit or make him afraid to do what he thought was right. He spoke openly against some of the religious leaders of his day and risked his life to preach the gospel, as he understood it. When he eventually died, it is said that one nobleman of his day looked down into Knox's open grave and said: 'Here lies one who never feared the face of man.' What an epitaph! What was this man's secret? Why did people say that he was fearless? His answer would have been, 'The Lord is my helper; I will not be afraid. What can man do to me?' (Hebrews 13:6).

TO THINK ABOUT

Do you have fears? How do you cope with them?

44

Welcome Friend!

FOCUS

Welcoming and accepting people just as they are.

SUMMARY

This assembly uses a story from the biography of the American Indian called Walking Buffalo, to show how we should treat everyone we meet with courtesy and consideration, whoever they are and whatever the colour of their skin.

RESOURCES

A 'Welcome' mat or a sign saying 'Welcome Friend'.

PREPARATION REQUIRED

None.

TALK

Some of you may have a mat outside your front door which has the word 'Welcome' written on it *(show mat if you have one)* or you may have seen a mat with this sign on it *(show sign)* 'Welcome Friend'.[1]

The message is clear, if you are a friend you are

welcome. It may also mean that you are welcome as a potential friend, even if you are not known to the people living in that house. But not everyone receives this kind of welcome from everyone they meet as the following story shows.

When white people first came to Canada, they often had a poor relationship with the American Indians they found there who had lived there for centuries. It was felt that education would help in promoting good relationships between the Indian tribes and the new white settlers. It was therefore decided to send an Indian boy called Walking Buffalo from the Stoney Indian Tribe to St John's College in Winnipeg. He had done well in his small local school but was bound to find it all very strange after life in his family's tepee on the small settlement.

Walking Buffalo found himself sharing a room with a white boy called Antony. From the start, Antony was hostile towards Walking Buffalo. He treated him with contempt and certainly did not put out any kind of 'welcome mat'. Instead he goaded Walking Buffalo with jibes like: 'Have you brought your bow and arrows with you?'

As time went on, Walking Buffalo settled into his new life and he began to show promise on the football field. This did not please Antony who continued to make Walking Buffalo's life as difficult as he could. His jealousy surfaced on the football field. Antony deliberately tripped Walking Buffalo up, sending him rolling across the field. As he got up, Walking Buffalo squared up to his old enemy. Antony landed him a heavy blow on the nose before Walking Buffalo could counter with a blow to the jaw which sent Antony flying.

The teacher came over to stop the fight going any further. He knew of the problems between the two boys and suggested that the only solution to their problem was to find Walking Buffalo a new room-mate. A Cree Indian boy was found to take Antony's place and peace was restored. Although Antony still harboured nasty thoughts towards Walking Buffalo, they generally kept away from one another as much as possible.

As winter passed and spring arrived, the ice on the Red River began to melt and Antony was determined to disregard the warnings about keeping well away from the river and on no account taking a canoe or boat out on it. Antony tried to persuade his friends to join him on a canoe trip down the river, but none of them wanted to take the risk. Undeterred, Antony set off on his own. He hadn't got far when he found his canoe being swept along by the strong current. He tried to go back, but the river was too strong and he was unable to fight against the current. He was now in serious danger.

As it happened, Walking Buffalo saw what was going on, and without any thought for his own safety he plunged into the freezing, muddy water and began to swim towards the helpless Antony. He managed to bring the canoe and Antony to shore.

By this time, a crowd of boys and teachers, including the headteacher, had gathered on the riverbank. They watched in disbelief. They realised that not only had Walking Buffalo shown great physical courage, but he had rescued a boy who had been his enemy since he entered the college. The headmaster held out his hand to Walking Buffalo, 'You're a hero,' he said, 'the school is proud of you.'

Once Antony had recovered from the shock of it all, he too finally recognised that he had been wrong about Walking Buffalo and had treated him very badly. He reached out his hand and said, 'I've been an ass, but if you can forgive me I'll try to be as good a man as you are. Thank you for treating me better than I deserve.'[2]

REFLECTION/RESPONSE

It is always easy to welcome people you like to be with and who you feel you can understand. It is not so easy to welcome others, but Christians believe that one should follow the example and teaching of Jesus who welcomed everyone who came to him. 'Come to me *all* you who are weary,' he said. His invitation includes everyone (Matthew 11:28).

TO THINK ABOUT

Does your friendship extend to everyone or do you leave some people out?

NOTES

1. Based on an original idea by David Hughes.
2. 'Chief Walking Buffalo' adapted from an extract from the biography by Grant MacEwan in D.M. Prescott, *Readings for the Senior Assembly* (Blandford Press: London, 1965).

45

Harvest

FOCUS

Harvest thanksgiving.

SUMMARY

In this assembly we look at the way a seed of corn is buried in the earth before sprouting and shooting up through the soil to produce a harvest. It compares this to the Christian idea of death and resurrection.

RESOURCES

A handful of corn seeds, a bunch of ripe corn, a loaf of bread and a child's lunchbox containing some sandwiches and a cake.

PREPARATION REQUIRED

None.

TALK

Once upon a time there was a mole who lived below the earth in a cornfield. Every day he spent his time looking for food and eating it. As soon as he finished breakfast he was searching out his lunch and as soon as he had eaten lunch he was looking for a tasty tea and then it would be time for supper. After supper he would take a stroll under the earth and work at extending his underground tunnel. Finally, exhausted by his efforts, he would curl up and fall asleep. The next morning it would all start again. Breakfast, lunch, tea, supper, tunnel-building and sleeping.

Then one day as he was taking his daily exercise he came across something rather strange. Everywhere he went there were seeds of corn buried in the earth. How peculiar, he thought, all these seeds just left in the soil. What a waste! Hundreds and hundreds of good seeds just going to waste! Of course, what the mole didn't realise was that the farmer had been busy sowing his corn *(show your handful of corn seeds)* that day in the hope that when the autumn came he would reap a good harvest.

For the next few weeks, the mole noticed how the corn seeds began to fall apart and wither up. Then he went away to another field for his summer holidays and forgot all about the poor seeds. When he came back, the first thing he noticed was that someone had been pushing a lot of sticks into the ground all across the old field. The seeds were gone, but now there were sticks everywhere he went under the earth. It was like walking through a forest. He didn't realise, of course, that the sticks had anything to do with the seeds of corn. He couldn't know that while he had been away, the seeds of corn had sprouted and grown pushing tall stalks of corn up through the soil. Above the ground, there was now a beautiful field of golden corn *(show bunch of ripe corn)* ripe and ready for cutting.

This story reminds Christians of something Jesus told his disciples. He said that he was like a corn of wheat which falls into the ground and dies before it brings forth a harvest (see John 12:24). His disciples couldn't believe that Jesus was going to die very soon. What a waste that would be. He was still quite a young man, why should he have to die? It didn't make sense. Jesus went on to show them that he must die in order to finish the work he had come to do and that they would eventually see and understand that through his death he would bring life to others.

In some of the poorer countries of the world which suffer from drought and a lack of rain to make the corn grow, people die because they have no corn and no other crops to harvest. They have no grain to sow the next year and no corn to grind up and make bread from to feed themselves and their families.

In this country, we can go into any bakery, supermarket or grocery store and buy bread. There are loaves like this one *(show your loaf of bread)* or you can choose from a range of different types of bread and rolls. There is white bread, brown bread, bread with seeds on and lots of different types of sliced loaves — thin-sliced, medium-sliced and thick-cut bread for toasting. So many sorts of bread!

Jesus also compared himself to a loaf of bread. He knew that his disciples might soon forget about the seeds of corn and the harvest fields and he wanted to leave them with a more powerful visual reminder of what his death would mean for them and for all those who believe in him. So, the night before he was arrested, taken for trial and condemned to death, he ate a final special meal with his disciples. At the end of the meal, he took a loaf of bread and broke it up. Then he handed the broken bread to his disciples and told them that when they ate bread in the future they should remember him and the way he laid down his life for them. Jesus knew that sharing their bread in this way would be a powerful reminder of his death and a clear picture of the way a seed of corn falls into the earth and dies before it brings forth a harvest.

REFLECTION/RESPONSE

Bread is something most of us would find hard to do without. Some of you will have had some bread or toast for your breakfast, perhaps with some jam or honey spread on it or with an egg. Some of you might have bread at teatime when you get home from school and some of you will have sandwiches or rolls for your lunch. You may have them carefully wrapped up and stored safely in a special lunchbox like this one *(show lunchbox and contents)*. You probably have your favourite sandwiches *(make some suggestions of what they might like in their sandwiches and show what you have in yours)* and you might have a lovely home-made cake or sticky bun. Great! I bet you would not be too keen on giving your lovely lunch away or having to share it with somebody else, would you? But you may remember a story in the Bible about a boy who went off one day with his packed lunch of five small loaves and two fishes — his favourite! He spent most of the day with a big crowd of people who had gathered to listen to a young preacher called Jesus. It was fascinating stuff and nobody wanted to go home, but most of them hadn't come prepared to stay the day and they were all getting very hungry. It was then that Jesus asked if anybody had brought any food. The boy thought about his rolls and fish, but thought they wouldn't go very far among so many people. Anyway, he decided to offer what he had and Jesus was pleased to accept it. After Jesus had given thanks for the boy's food, the disciples started to hand it out to the crowd. Incredibly, it just kept going until everyone had some!

Perhaps this harvest-time there is a special lesson in this story for all of us. Jesus could not have fed all those people that day if the boy had not come forward with his lunch. It wasn't much, but it was all he had. When we see pictures on our TV and in the newspapers about the people in the Sudan or in other poor countries where they are starving because there is no harvest and no food, we may think that there is nothing we can do about it. Well, there is. We can offer what we can. It may not seem much, just a few pence or some items for a fund-raising effort, but when we all put what we can give together, it can become something of real value.

TO THINK ABOUT

What have you got to offer the poor, the malnourished and the starving in the world this harvest-time? Perhaps pupils can come up with some fund-raising ideas to support a suitable current/ ongoing project to feed people whose harvest has failed and who are on the brink of a humanitarian disaster.

46

Remembrance Day

FOCUS

Gratitude for the sacrifice of so many people.

SUMMARY

This assembly centres on one man's personal story of World War 2. It shows something of what going off to war meant for Frank and his family. It invites pupils to reflect on the cost of war in human terms.

RESOURCES

A map to help show all the countries Frank went to as a soldier.

PREPARATION REQUIRED

None.

TALK

Some of you may know someone who is in the army, navy or airforce. If you do, you will know that sometimes they are sent to another country like Bosnia or the Falkland Islands to serve their country.

This may mean helping to keep the peace by keeping two opposing sides apart or it may mean that they get caught up in the fighting themselves. It is often dangerous work and it can be a very worrying time for their families.

Frank had only been married ten days when he got his call-up papers. It was March 1940. Britain was at war with Germany and Frank was needed to fight for his country. He joined the 17th Middlesex Regiment in the 51st Highland Division. Frank's was the only English Regiment in the Highland Division. After a few weeks of training, Frank was sent up to Scotland to join the 51st Highland Division. Here Frank and his companions boarded the ship that was to take them to Durban in South Africa and from there to the Middle East. The ship finally docked at Port Said and the last part of this long journey — a lorry ride that ended in the Egyptian desert.

Here they had to 'dig in' which meant digging the trenches where they would live for the next month. During the day they would lie flat in the trenches to avoid enemy fire as best they could and try to sleep. At night they would take turns doing guard duty and other chores.

In October 1940, at Alamein, the biggest bombardment of the War began and the British guns went into action. Frank was ordered to advance behind the big guns towards enemy lines. They were under fire for most of this time and there were many casualties. Up ahead, tank battles were taking place between the German Army and the British Eighth Army, which was under the command of General Montgomery. They were dangerous times. After about five weeks the British forces broke through enemy lines, and from there, Frank went on with the remaining members of his regiment to Tripoli, Libya (where Winston Churchill addressed them) and from there to Algeria where they met up with the 1st Army.

After more training, Frank was sent with his company to Sicily to take part in the invasion. They crossed the Mediterranean in American-built 'Liberty Boats' as they were called. These were craft that had been welded together rather than riveted and they did not cope well with the fierce storm that blew up on the crossing. Everyone was seasick and could have done little to fight back if an enemy strike had occurred. There was only light resistance to the invading forces in Sicily, and for the next three months Frank was billeted in a village near Mount Etna. He spent much of his time here as driver for the Platoon Commander, Lieutenant Cavendish. Frank then took the chance to return to Britain as part of the advance party whose job it would be to make preparations for the return of the rest of the regiment. Over two years after setting sail for the Middle East, Frank was back in Scotland. The group boarded a train for St Albans where they had to report before they could go on leave. One of the group actually lived near the Clyde and the train passed by the end of his garden on its way to St Albans. You can guess how he felt as he saw his home from the train and there, to his amazement, was his wife hanging out the washing. Shout and wave as he did, he could not make her hear. Of course, none of the families knew their loved ones were coming home and it was the next day before the soldier could get the train back home to be reunited with his wife after nearly two and a half years away.

Frank too, was looking forward to seeing his wife and family. He got the first bus he could to his home in Walthamstow in East London. It was a Sunday in the summer of 1942. Sadly, the war was not over and Frank had to return to the fighting. After further training with the rest of the battalion, Frank found himself in Tilbury where, on 5 June 1943, he left for France and the 'D' Day Invasion (6 June 1943) which was to mark the start of some of the fiercest fighting of the War.

As they went ashore, Frank was at the wheel of a truck loaded with ammunition and supplies. As they pushed forward, Frank took his turn manning the machine guns and driving the Bren Gun Carriers. Frank saw action in Normandy, Belgium and Holland. When thousands of paratroopers were dropped near Arnhem, Frank's company was ordered forward to try to reach them, but they could not get through. Many lives were lost there. Then, when the German Army broke through in the Ardennes, Frank was sent to Germany. It was Christmas and bitterly cold dug in behind the American forces.

After the fighting died down there, Frank was sent back to the Rhine for the final push across the river and into Germany itself. The cease-fire came as Frank reached Hamburg. Frank recalls the terrible devastation that met his eyes as he entered the city. Large areas of Hamburg had been completely flattened by the bombing. It was something Frank would never forget.

REFLECTION/RESPONSE

There are many incidents which still stand out in Frank's mind over fifty years on. One of the worst memories Frank has is of seeing people who had been released from the concentration camp that he passed on his way to Hamburg. The other memory is of seeing row upon row of refugees, mostly women and children, fleeing the fighting. They were making their way back along the road Frank had travelled, carrying what they could in bundles and on carts and in prams. It was a terrible sight.

There were many very frightening times too. One

of the most frightening for Frank was when they were 'dive bombed' while 'dug in' at Alamein. The noise was terrifying and shells were exploding all around them. Frank thought he had been hit. He could feel something cold running down his back and he asked his friend to check it out. It turned out that the water tank behind them had been hit, and water from the leaking tank was spilling into the trench where they were standing, but it had been a close call!

There were some happy memories too. After the cease-fire, Frank was billeted in a school in Hamburg. As Christmas approached, the head-teacher asked Frank and his friend if they would like to come down to hear the children sing a carol. They did, and it was hard to hide one's emotions as the children sang their carefully rehearsed version of the carol 'Silent Night'.

Frank spent the first six years of his married life in the army serving his country. His young daughter didn't know him when he came home, but Frank counts himself as one of the lucky ones — he was one of the few from his regiment who came back.

Remembrance Day is a time when Frank and his family think back especially to the War years. He remembers friends and colleagues he fought alongside and he remembers those who did not survive the War, but who paid the supreme sacrifice.

Let us remember too, and let us never forget that we owe a great debt of gratitude to all those men and women who gave so much to win for us the freedom we enjoy today.

TO THINK ABOUT

How do you think you would have coped if you had been Frank? How would you have felt being sent off to war just ten days after you had been married? How would you have coped if you had been left at home as Frank's wife was?

47

Advent Light

FOCUS

Light as a symbol of Advent.

SUMMARY

This assembly looks at different ideas associated with light. It shows how Christians see Advent as a time of waiting for the light of Christ to come into the world.

RESOURCES

One large thick and one small thin candle, plus a variety of different shaped and coloured candles. Include a perfumed candle and a cake candle.

PREPARATION REQUIRED

None.

TALK

Today I have brought in some candles to show you *(show candles and light them as you are talking).* Can anyone tell me what the differences are between these candles? *(Draw out ideas about their size, shape, smell, the amount of light they give, etc.)* What do we use these candles for? *(Eg celebrations, birthdays,*

emergencies when the electricity supply is cut off, etc.)
Of course, years ago before electricity was available, people used lamps and candles as their main source of light. In some schools, children had to take their own candle along and place it on their desks so that in the dark winter days they had just enough light to be able to see to do their work. Of course, not everyone was able to go to school in those days, and for some it meant walking several miles to get there.

There is a story about two boys who lived high up in the Alps in Switzerland. One was called Hans and the other was called Karl. They were great friends and they always walked to school together. Their school was five miles away, so it meant they had to get up very early to get there on time and in the winter months it was always dark when they set out and dark by the time they got home. They carried their school books tied together with a strap and in their hand each boy carried a candle. The candles the pupils brought with them were the only means of light in the school. As each boy arrived, they would stamp the snow from their boots and set their candle down on their desks. By the time every pupil had arrived, the whole room would be a blaze of light. The teacher had no problem calling the register there, because he could see immediately if a light was missing. No candle — no boy. It might be that the missing boys had been snowed up or that they had been forced to return home because of poor weather or it might be that that pupil was ill or had simply decided not to go to school that day.

One day, as Karl and Hans were walking to school in the darkness of a cold winter morning, they had a quarrel. It wasn't really about anything very much, but they said some bitter things to each other. Eventually, Hans said that he didn't want to walk any further with Karl. He was going to take the shorter route, over the frozen river. This was a much more dangerous path, and they had been told never to go that way in the winter months. There were no posts to mark the way and one could easily get lost in the deep snow.

Karl went on alone and arrived safely at the school. He sat down at his desk and lit up his candle. There was no light on the desk next to him and no sign of Hans. Without saying anything, Karl got up, put his boots and heavy coat on again, and struck out back along the path until he came to the point where the boys had parted company. It was getting light now, so Karl was able to see the footprints left by Hans. He crossed the frozen river — still no sign of Hans. Eventually, two miles from the school, Karl found Hans, lying asleep in the frozen snow, still clutching his candle, but overcome by exhaustion, and lost. The snow was beginning to drift over him, but using his bare hands, Karl dug Hans out and hoisted him onto his shoulders. He carried him the two miles to the school and into the safety and light of the classroom.

Soon, both boys were back at their desks, candles alight and working hard at their studies. Hans had a thick candle on his desk (rather like this one) because his parents were well off and could afford the best. Karl, on the other hand, only had a smaller thin candle (like this). It was the smallest candle in the room because his mother was quite poor and couldn't afford anything better. This did not stop Karl from working hard, however, and in time he passed all his exams and went on to become a doctor. Eventually, he went to Italy where people were dying because of a terrible epidemic that had broken out there. The poor people there had no access to a doctor and Karl decided that this was what he wanted to do. After saving many lives, Karl finally caught the plague himself. In his weakness and with a high fever, Karl thought he was back trudging through the deep snow to get to school. But this time, he had forgotten to bring his candle. The old school master was saying to him, 'Never mind, Karl, you won't need it today. There is plenty of light where you are going.' For Christians, heaven is a place of great light. There is no need for candles there or light from the sun, because God is light. For Christians, Jesus is light and at Advent Christians look forward to Christmas as the time when God sent his Son to bring light into this dark world.

REFLECTION/RESPONSE

In the ancient city of Verona in northern Italy, there are the remains of a huge Roman amphitheatre. In the summer months, the amphitheatre becomes the setting for a series of operas. People flock to Verona to see and hear the opera from all over the world. As they go into the arena, people are handed a small candle (some people bring their own). People are seated on the stone steps that encircle the stage. Finally, just before the performance begins and darkness falls, people light up their candles. The arena becomes a sea of little lights. Then, as the light of the candles begins to fade, the huge stage lights come on and the opera begins.

One tiny candle in that huge arena would have very little effect. The light given by Karl and Hans's candles in that old schoolroom wasn't very great on its own either, but all these lights together made a real impact.

Perhaps we think that any light we can bring into this dark world will be of little effect, but what we need to remember this Advent time is that if we shine together we can make a real impact and bring light and happiness to those around us.

TO THINK ABOUT

What other symbols are there for Advent?

48

Angelology

FOCUS

Angels.

SUMMARY

This assembly looks at some references to angels in the Bible and centres on the relevance of angels to the Christmas story.

RESOURCES

OHT of the angel drawing and any other pictures of angels, Christmas cards with angels on and any angel Christmas decoration or ornamental angel.

PREPARATION REQUIRED

Four pupils to practise the Bible readings.

TALK

Over the Christmas period we hear a lot about angels. There are angels in the Christmas story — one appeared to Mary and a whole crowd sang to the shepherds. There are angels in the shops, not real ones of course, but china ones, tinsel ones and cut-out ones *(show angels)*. There are pictures of

angels on Christmas cards *(show cards)* and children dressed up as angels in nativity plays. Angels everywhere! Why this sudden interest in angels? We don't seem to hear much about them for the rest of the year! If you went around asking people if they believed in angels, most of them would probably hesitate or say 'no', but they don't mind them being part of a colourful festival like Christmas. That's different! But the truth is that the Bible has quite a lot to say about angels and they are not just associated with the Christmas story as you will see. But first, let's see how much you know about angels in this special angelology quiz.

ANGELOLOGY QUIZ:

1. What does the word 'angel' mean?

   Answer: It means 'messenger'. According to the Bible, angels are messengers of God (see Luke 1:11–13, 18,19).

2. Do angels have wings?

   Answer: We can't be sure if they have wings as such, but they do have some kind of supernatural means of movement. The angel Gabriel, for example, came swiftly to the prophet Daniel and instructed him (Daniel 9:21). The archangel Michael is seen to fight on behalf of the people of God (Jude 9; Daniel 10:13,21; Revelation 12:7). Zechariah also talked with an angel (Luke 1:11–20).

3. Do angels die?

   Answer: No. They are immortal (Luke 20:35–36).

4. What do angels do?

   Answer: They praise God and do errands for him (Isaiah 6:2–3; Hebrews 1:14; Luke 2:13–14; Daniel 6:22; Acts 12:7–8).

5. Do people become angels when they die?

   Answer: No. Angels are heavenly beings with special services to perform. Sometimes, as special

messengers, they are sent directly by God (Genesis 32:1–2; Exodus 3:2; Hebrews 1:7).
6. Are angels to be worshipped?
Answer: No. Only God is to be worshipped (see Revelation 22:8–9).
7. What have angels got to do with us?
Answer: Many Bible scholars believe that the Bible indicates that each of us has our own personal guardian angel (Matthew 18:10).
8. What part did angels play in Jesus' earthly life?
Answer: They 'ministered' to him (Matthew 4:11; 26:53; Luke 22:43). They were also present at his resurrection, ascension and will be at his second coming (John 20:12; Acts 1:11; Matthew 25:31).

The Bible also tells us that angels are glad and rejoice when a person acknowledges Jesus as the Christ.

The Christmas story mentions angels several times (put up OHT). The first occasion is when the angel Gabriel is sent by God to Mary to tell her that she has been chosen to be the mother of the Lord. Here is the account of this story from Luke's Gospel.

Reader 1: Luke 1:26–37.

The second time an angel is mentioned in the story about Jesus' birth is when an angel appears to Joseph in a dream.

Reader 2: Matthew 1:18–21.

Angels also appear to the shepherds to tell them the news about Jesus' birth.

Reader 3: Luke 2:8–15.

Finally, after the visit of the Wise Men, Joseph is warned by an angel to leave his homeland and go down to Egypt to escape the wrath of King Herod.

Reader 4: Matthew 2:13–15.

REFLECTION/RESPONSE

Angels are an important part of the Christmas story, but many people put angels on the same level as Santa Claus — a harmless and pleasant fairy tale. What do you think? Do you believe in angels?

TO THINK ABOUT

How many carols can you name that have something about angels in them?

49

What Do You Want for Christmas?

FOCUS

Christmas as a time for giving and receiving.

SUMMARY

This assembly uses the age-old question of what pupils want for Christmas as a jumping-off point. It then encourages them to think about what they want most in life.

RESOURCES

A number of gift-wrapped boxes labelled with things like a sense of humour, wisdom, and other qualities.

PREPARATION REQUIRED

The above visual aids.

Do you realise that there are only a few shopping days left until Christmas? It's that time of the year when we have to start getting ready for the big event and think about what we are going to get for everybody this year. Perhaps you have already got all your presents, but some of us are probably still thinking about what we can get certain people who seem to have everything. Sometimes I resort to asking people what they want because I can't think of anything to buy them.

One of the things I enjoy about Christmas is taking my children/grandchildren/god children/nieces/ nephews to visit Father Christmas. It's great to have an excuse to explore Santa's grotto and meet all his helpers! One thing I would love to do is go to Lapland and take a sleigh ride to meet the real Father Christmas — well, wouldn't you? That would be really something!

Perhaps you can remember being taken to visit Santa in his grotto when you were small. Usually, Santa lifts the children onto his knee and then asks them age-old questions: 'Have you been a good boy/ girl this year?' 'Well then, what would you like for Christmas?' Imagine Santa turns to you and asks that question: 'What do you want for Christmas?' I wonder what you would reply.

There is an interesting story in the Bible about a man called Caleb who posed a similar question to Achsah. In his younger days, Joshua had chosen Caleb, the Hebrew leader, to go into Canaan to spy out the land. When others came back with stories about giants and feeling like 'grasshoppers in their sight', Caleb was full of the wonders he had seen and reports of a 'land flowing with milk and honey'. As a reward, when the Jews conquered Canaan, Caleb was given some land around Hebron, although it was left to him to drive out the people already settled there. This he did, but when it came to attacking the city of Debir, he decided to offer the hand of his daughter Achsah to the man who could take this city. The man who led a successful attack against Debir was Othniel. So, true to his word, Caleb gave his permission for Othniel to marry his daughter. He also gave them a plot of land as a wedding present.

Everything seemed in order and the marriage took place, but Achsah was still not happy. One day she came to her father with a request. Falling on her knees before him, she made her case. Achsah said that they were grateful for the southlands Caleb had given them, but it was a dry, arid country. There were no wells and no springs of water there. Caleb could no doubt see the problem, but he wanted Achsah to tell him what she wanted him to do about it. 'What do you wish?' he asked her. 'What do you want?' In response Achsah asked for a spring of water, so Caleb gave them the upper and the lower springs.[1]

What would you say if you were asked the same question? What do you wish — or — what do you want for Christmas? Imagine you could have any-thing you wanted. I wonder what you would ask for?

When Jesus was born he received some unusual gifts. The Wise Men brought him presents of gold, frankincense and myrrh. Each of these gifts was symbolic. The gold was a symbol of kingship. The frankincense spoke of the divine, priestly role of Jesus as frankincense was used in making incense that was burnt in the Temple of God. Myrrh was a symbol of suffering because it was mixed with aloes and used in the preparation of Christ's body for bur-ial. They were strange gifts, but full of meaning. We do not know what happened to them. Perhaps Mary kept them, or perhaps not being a wealthy family, they used them when they were needed.

REFLECTION/RESPONSE

For Christians, Christmas is about a very special gift, God's gift of his Son to the world. It is also a time for celebrating this gift by giving to others. If you could have anything you wanted, including the things that money couldn't buy, I wonder what you would wish for? If you could choose between a mountain bike, computer or some of the gifts I have here, I wonder which you would choose? *(Bring out gift-wrapped boxes appropriately labelled.)* Do you wish you had a good sense of humour, a generous spirit, more wisdom, etc?

I wonder, what do you want for Christmas? Probably, the older you get the harder it is to answer that question. An American TV presenter, who had the money to buy whatever he wanted, commented on the fact that when most people are asked what they want for Christmas they usually answer with something material. But as one of the people who can afford to buy anything he wants, he finds that what he really, really wants, he cannot buy — ie things like love, real friendship and peace of mind. What do you want for Christmas?

TO THINK ABOUT

What do you think happened to the gifts of gold, frankincense and myrrh brought to Jesus by the Wise Men?

NOTES
1. Joshua 15:13–19.

50

<u>THEME</u>

A Special Meal

FOCUS

Passover and The Last Supper.

SUMMARY

This assembly uses the idea of sharing a special meal with family or friends as a way into looking at the last meal Jesus had with his disciples and the relevance of that to Christians today.

RESOURCES

A loaf of bread or a Matzoth and a glass of red wine or grape juice. Three pupils for the sketch.

PREPARATION REQUIRED

Practice for the pupils involved in the sketch.

TALK

Most of us enjoy a good meal. Even better, a special meal that marks a special occasion. Christmas dinner is probably one of the highlights of our culinary calendar! There is plenty to eat and lots of fun and laughter. The table will probably be loaded with food. At Christmas there's the turkey, roast potatoes,

lots of vegetables, stuffing, bread sauce, and to follow — Christmas pudding! On your birthday, you
will probably have a special cake with candles and
you might get to choose your favourite foods or go
to your favourite eating place or fast food restaurant. Whatever meal you have, it will be a special
time of celebration and an opportunity to share the
occasion with others. Eating together also gives us a
chance to talk to one another and enjoy one
another's company. Birthdays and Christmas are
also about giving and receiving presents and showing people close to us how much we care about and
appreciate them.

Of course, birthdays and Christmas may not be
the only times we get together with friends and
family for a special meal. Sometimes we have a special meal to celebrate an anniversary of some sort or
a special achievement, like passing an exam or getting a new job. Occasionally, we might have a special meal to say goodbye to someone who is moving
home or going to a different school or job.

Jesus shared a goodbye meal with his disciples on
the last night before he was arrested and put to
death on a cross. This meal is often known as the
Last Supper for that reason. It was a very special
occasion, but it was a sad time too, because Jesus
knew what was about to happen to him.

Let's take an imaginary trip back through time
now and hear about the events of that night from
our reporter Joseph Ben Hur, who is in Jerusalem
with some of Jesus' friends who were with him that
night.

Reporter: Yes. Thank you. Well, I'm standing in the
heart of the old city of Jerusalem quite close to the
area where the meal took place. People seem to be
going about their business here much as usual this
morning after the traumatic events of last week.

With me are two people who were very close to the man from Galilee and they are Peter and John. Thank you for taking the time to be with us this morning. Let me ask you first, Peter, what happened exactly?

Peter: Well, Joseph, it was a remarkable night. John and I had been in the city earlier that day to make preparations for the meal and see things were organised for the evening. We knew that Jesus was in a lot of danger, although we didn't realise just how much. So, it came as no surprise to us that he had made special arrangements for us to eat the Passover meal at a secret location where the risk of arrest was not so great.

Reporter: You say it was a secret location. So how did you know where to take the food and get the meal ready?

Peter: Good question! Jesus told us that when we came into the city, we were to look for a man carrying a water pot and follow him. He would lead us to the place where we were to make the meal ready.

Reporter: Some of our listeners might not realise, of course, that it is very unusual to see a man carrying the water as this is a job usually done by women or donkeys! So, what happened next?

Peter: Well, we followed this chap to an enclosed area quite near the city wall and then he left us with the doorman who showed us to the upstairs room which had been reserved for us.

Reporter: Sounds real 'cloak and dagger' stuff. Were you afraid of being arrested yourself?

Peter: Not really. I don't think that we had any idea then what was about to take place over the next twenty-four hours.

Reporter: Let me turn to you now, John. You were there with Peter helping to get things ready for the evening meal I understand. What reason did Jesus give for wanting to have this meal and for going to all this trouble? Was it a special occasion?

John: Well, yes it was. As you know it was Passover last week, and it was a Passover meal that Peter and I prepared. We didn't know then that it was going to be anything more than that.

Reporter: Just explain very briefly what a Passover meal is for people who are not familiar with it, could you please?

John: Sure. Passover is a Jewish festival to commemorate the time when God delivered our ancestors, the Hebrews, from years of slavery in Egypt. God sent ten plagues on the Egyptians to persuade them that they should release all their Hebrew slaves and allow them to go to a new land where they would be free to worship God in their own way.

Reporter: So let me get this right. You have a special meal every year at Passover time to celebrate the release of your ancestors from slavery in Egypt, and that's what you were doing on the night in question?

John: Exactly right. When Jesus and the rest of the group arrived we had everything set up for a Passover meal.

Reporter: If I can come back to you now, Peter. I understand things were a little different that night though.

Peter: Yes. I admit I wasn't too happy when Jesus offered the best seats at the table to John and Judas and I was left to find my own. Silly really, but I imagined having got things ready with John that he and I would sit either side of Jesus as his right-hand and left-hand men, so to speak. I couldn't believe it when he asked Judas to be on his left.

John: That's true. I was shocked as well and I felt a bit awkward as Peter had done as much work as I had. Anyway, we went through the meal as usual, except Jesus kept saying that someone in the room was about to betray him to the authorities. We couldn't believe it. One of his own group, a close friend, betray him? It seemed absurd. Anyway, Judas went out some time after that and it turned out to be him. Mind you, he always seemed to be a bit of the odd one out.

Reporter: I understand this must be a bit upsetting for you, but can you just tell us what happened at the end of the meal?

Peter: Yes. Well, Jesus took some of the unleavened bread that we always have at Passover, and broke it and handed it round. He said something like: 'This is my body, broken for you. Do this to remember me.' It was all very sombre. I realise now that Jesus was telling us that he was about to be put to death on the cross and that we should remember this every time we sat down to share the bread together.

Reporter: He also gave a new significance to the wine, I understand, John.

John: That's right. He took a cup of wine and said that it represented a new covenant or agreement, which would be written in blood — his blood, of course, and that we were to share the wine like that in memory of him along with the broken bread. It was a very moving moment. After that, we all sang a Passover song and went out to the Garden of Gethsemane where Jesus was arrested after a tip-off from Judas.

Reporter: Thank you both very much for sharing that with us. We've run out of time now, so I'll have to hand back to the studio. Joseph Ben Hur. News East, Jerusalem.

REFLECTION/RESPONSE

Thank you for that very clear insight into the events of that evening which are still remembered almost 2,000 years later by Christians all over the world. In a simple service, often called the Eucharist, Communion or Last Supper, Christians share the bread *(show)* and the wine *(show)* in the way Jesus asked them to do, as powerful reminders of his death and resurrection.

Let's think about the story we have heard and the significance of the broken bread and the shared cup of wine in a moment of quiet reflection.

TO THINK ABOUT

What made that meal such a special one for Jesus, his disciples and Christians today?

51

THEME

New Year

FOCUS

Looking backward, going forwards.

SUMMARY

This assembly invites pupils to put aside past failures, try to learn from their mistakes and look to the future.

RESOURCES

Rubbish bin or sack. Some large sheets of paper on which are written some of last year's failures or things that pupils might like to forget or be able to put behind them (eg a poor test mark, a quarrel with a friend, a sad event, a lost opportunity). A suitcase in which to place the things to carry with you into a New Year (eg a sense of humour, a generous spirit).

PREPARATION REQUIRED

Write above captions and find a rubbish sack and suitcase. Prepare pupils for the sketches.

TALK

Imagine for a moment that at the start of every new year, you could gather up all the things that have spoilt it or held you back in the past year and throw them away in this sack *(two pupils to hold up sack)*. Then they would be taken away to the nearest rubbish tip so that you would never be able to drag them up or be made to remember them again. If we could get rid of past mistakes or past concerns in this way, I wonder what things you would want to throw away and never be reminded about again? Here are a few ideas:

(Each caption is held up as pupils come out in pairs to enact each problem.)

1. A poor test mark

Pupil 1: What's the matter with you?

Pupil 2: I messed up my maths test.

Pupil 1: Yeh? What did you get?

Pupil 2: I scored a miserable 25%. Not even a pass mark.

Pupil 1: Well, it's not that bad. You should try and forget about it now. If you work at it, I'm sure you will do better next time.

Pupil 2: I suppose so.

Pupil 1: Come on then. Let's get rid of it!

(They take the caption, screw it up and stuff it into the bin or rubbish sack.)

2. A quarrel with a friend

(Pupil 1 and 2 enter, arguing.)

Pupil 1: I don't care! Whatever you say now, I know you don't mean it.

Pupil 2: I do! Look I'm really sorry, OK? I don't know why I grassed you up like that.

Pupil 1: Well you did, and I don't see how I can ever trust you again.

Pupil 2: Just give me a chance will you? I promise I won't let you down. Please!!

Pupil 1: All right. I'll forget it this time. I don't like us not being friends either.

(They throw the appropriate caption into the bin/sack together.)

3. A sad event

Pupil 1: If only I'd made sure the door of the hutch was shut properly I'm sure Bugsy wouldn't have got out and disappeared like that.

Pupil 2: O come on, Mary. You don't know it was you anyway. Anyone could have done it. You know what your brother's like. It might have been him.

Pupil 1: It doesn't help telling me that. I know it was me and now I'll never see Bugsy again.

Pupil 2: Well, I think you should stop going over and over it and blaming yourself all the time. You can't do anything about it now, nothing will bring Bugsy back.

Pupil 1: I suppose you're right. It's time to put it behind me now.

(Pupil 1 throws caption into sack/bin.)

4. A lost opportunity

Pupil 1: If only I'd taken the time to sit down and listen, I might have been able to do something about it.

Pupil 2: True. But then none of us realised how serious the problem was then, did we?

Pupil 1: No. But that's just my point. We knew he was upset about something, but none of us bothered to find out what the problem was. If we had, things might have turned out differently.

Pupil 2: Well, it's too late to do anything about it now. We'll just have to put it down to experience and do better next time.

(Pupil 2 consigns the caption to the bin.)

RESUME TALK

You may not have experienced any of these things, but I'm sure that we have all done or experienced things in the past that we need to put behind us. That may mean putting things right with someone we have had a disagreement with. It may mean working harder. It may be that we have to learn from the experience and try not to make the same mistake again. Whatever it is, we need to see the beginning of a new year as a chance to make a fresh start. We need to seize the opportunity to 'pick ourselves up, dust ourselves off and start all over again'. Instead of looking back and continuing to harbour regrets about things in the past that we can't change or do anything about now, let's look to the future and think about the sort of things we can do.

(Produce empty suitcase and have captions ready to put into the case as you go through them.)

Things to take with us into a new year:

- *A sense of humour.* We won't get very far without being able to sit back and laugh at ourselves occasionally.

- *A generous spirit.* Better to think of others and offer a helping hand when it's needed than thinking only of ourselves and what we can get out of something.

- *The determination to use time wisely.* No more

time-wasting! That's not to say we never take time to rest or relax and enjoy ourselves, but it does mean wasting less time and thinking more about what we do with the time we have.

- *A forgiving nature.* People are bound to do things that will upset us, but forgiveness is free. Let's try to be more forgiving in the future and spend less time harbouring grudges or ill will towards others who have hurt us in some way.

- *Honesty.* No one likes a person who can't be trusted. Our word should be our bond.

- *The ability to keep our promises.* How often have we said things or made a commitment that we haven't been able to keep? No more making promises we can't keep or letting people down.

A new year offers all of us an opportunity to look back at the past, try to learn from it and then put it behind us and move forward. Let's determine that this year will be the best that we can make it.

REFLECTION/RESPONSE

Lord, we ask your forgiveness for the past and your blessing and forgiveness for the future. Forgive us for the mistakes in the past and opportunities not taken. As we go into a new year, give us a spirit of adventure and a determination to do what we know is right. Amen.

TO THINK ABOUT

What things do you need to put behind you and what qualities do you think you will need to meet the challenges of the year ahead?

52

Easter

FOCUS

Personal sacrifice.

SUMMARY

This assembly looks at the message of supreme sacrifice that underlies the Christian festival of Easter. It begins with the true story of a parachute instructor who saved the life of a trainee by sacrificing his own life. It goes on to apply this story to the message of Easter and Jesus' sacrifice of his own life on the cross.

RESOURCES

OHT of the drawing of the two parachutists harnessed together.

PREPARATION REQUIRED

None.

TALK

What is the most exciting thing you have ever done? What is the most thrilling thing you would like to do? Some of you have probably been on

some very scary rides at one of the big funfairs or parks *(an example of a local attraction could be given here)*. Perhaps you have jumped off a high diving board or been out in a speed boat. Some people get their thrills from things like bungee jumping or doing a charity parachute jump *(perhaps a member of staff has done or is planning something like this!)*. Gareth Griffiths, a twenty-seven-year-old management consultant, decided to take up sky diving as a way of getting a thrill. So he signed up for a two-week course with the Paragators parachute school at Umatilla Airport in America.

His jump from 13,000 feet up should have been the first of twenty he and his five friends were due to make. Gareth was third to go. He was strapped firmly to the shoulders and waist of his forty-seven-year-old instructor, Mike Costello, as this picture shows *(put up OHT of drawing)*. They stepped out of the small Cessna aircraft into clear blue skies. Harnessed together, the pair began to hurtle towards the earth below. The small drogue parachute attached to the instructor's back opened normally. This would keep their speed to 125 miles per hour. Forty seconds later, at 6,000 feet, Mike pulled the ripcord to release the main chute. It failed to open properly. Mike reached out for the reserve chute, but it too refused to open properly and became entangled with the main chute. The pair were plummeting towards the earth at a frightening speed. Onlookers watched in horror as they saw the pair fall to the ground beyond a perimeter hedge. They ran to the spot expecting to find both men dead. Instead, they found Gareth alive and conscious still strapped to his instructor, Mike Costello, who lay dead beneath him.

It later emerged that brave Mike had deliberately changed places with Gareth as they had plummeted to earth in order to cushion the impact of Gareth's fall. In a split-second decision, 100 feet above the ground, Mike had decided to manipulate the steering toggle as they fell so that he was able to swing his own body underneath Gareth, taking the impact of the fall. The owner of the Paragators school said that Mike must have known what he was doing, and that he must have made a deliberate decision to save the life of his pupil by sacrificing his own. Mike had made over 7,500 jumps, 2,000 of them in tandem, but this was to be his last. Gareth was taken to the Orlando Regional Medical Centre where he underwent a successful operation to fuse together his fractured spine and was expected to make a good recovery.

REFLECTION/RESPONSE

The headline in one national paper read: 'Hug of a hero saves para plunge Briton'. Gareth had fallen two miles, but lived to tell the tale because of one brave man's supreme sacrifice.

This story may remind you of other stories where people have sacrificed their own lives to save someone else. One story about a young man who paid the supreme price to save the lives of others is found in the Bible. It is the story of how Jesus went to the cross and died in order to save others who would believe in him and put their trust in him. Christians believe that Jesus took the sins of the world upon his shoulders by sacrificing his own life on the cross. For Christians, this is the basis of their faith and the message of Easter as expressed in the prayer below:

Dear God

Thank you for sending your Son, Jesus, into the world to die on the cross. Help us to remember the way you gave your life to save ours. Thank you for the joy of Easter and the way we celebrate it with chocolate eggs and special food. Thank you for the hope Easter brings and the promise of new life. Amen.

TO THINK ABOUT

How can you show your love and concern for the people you care about?

NOTES
My special thanks to Scarlett Kilden for the Easter prayer.